PUPIL TEXTBOOK 5A

Noogol

Googol

Koogol

Ooogol

Toogol

Zoogol

Consultant and author
Dr Fong Ho Kheong

Authors
Gan Kee Soon and Chelvi Ramakrishnan

UK consultants
Carole Skinner, Simon d'Angelo and Elizabeth Gibbs

© 2015 Marshall Cavendish Education Pte Ltd

Published by Marshall Cavendish Education
Times Centre, 1 New Industrial Road, Singapore 536196
Customer Service Hotline: (65) 6213 9444
Email: tmesales@mceducation.com
Website: www.mceducation.com

Distributed by
Oxford University Press
Great Clarendon Street, Oxford,
OX2 6DP, United Kingdom
www.oxfordprimary.co.uk
www.oxfordowl.co.uk

First published 2015
Reprinted 2015, 2016

ISBN 978-981-01-8895-5

Printed in China

Acknowledgements
Written by Dr Fong Ho Kheong, Gan Kee Soon and Chelvi Ramakrishnan

UK consultants: Carole Skinner, Simon d'Angelo and Elizabeth Gibbs

Cover artwork by Daron Parton

The authors and publisher would like to thank all schools and individuals
who helped to trial and review Inspire Maths resources.

Introduction

Inspire Maths is a comprehensive, activity-based programme designed to provide pupils with a firm foundation in maths and to develop the creative and critical thinking skills to become fluent problem solvers.

Inspire Maths makes learning maths fun and rewarding through the use of engaging illustrations and games that help to reinforce and consolidate learning.

For the teacher:

Use the engaging and highly scaffolded **Let's Learn!** to introduce concepts. Integrated questions allow for immediate assessment and consolidation of concepts learnt.

Carry out investigative activities in **Let's Explore!** These allow pupils to apply concepts learnt.

Challenge pupils to solve non-routine questions by applying relevant heuristics and thinking skills in **Put On Your Thinking Caps!**

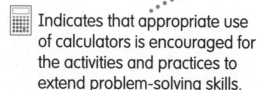 Indicates that appropriate use of calculators is encouraged for the activities and practices to extend problem-solving skills.

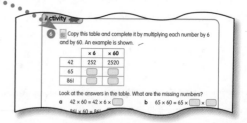

For the parent/guardian:

Home Maths

Build home-school links and make maths come alive by using the tips in Home Maths to help children apply mathematical concepts to daily life.

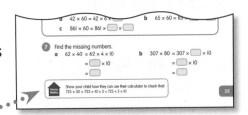

For the pupil:

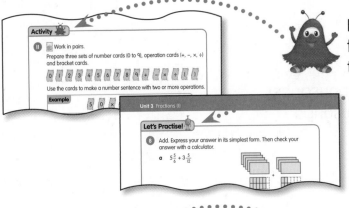

Enjoy **Inspire Maths** with your friends. Explore your learning through activities and group work.

Let's Practise! contains questions that provide opportunities for further practice.

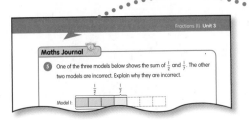

Share what you have learnt, create your own questions and become aware of your own mathematical thinking in your **Maths Journal**.

Recall skills from earlier years and link them to new concepts in the current unit.

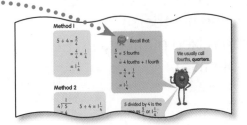

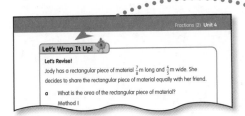

Let's Wrap It Up! summarises the concepts you have learnt in the current unit, while **Let's Revise!** provides a worked example that covers the key concepts for ease of revision.

Contents

Whole Numbers (I)

Let's Learn!

Numbers to 10 million

1 Count in ten thousands.

1 ten thousand (10 000), 2 ten thousands (20 000), 3 ten thousands (30 000), 4 ten thousands (40 000), 5 ten thousands (50 000), 6 ten thousands (60 000), 7 ten thousands (70 000), 8 ten thousands (80 000), 9 ten thousands (90 000),
☐.

> Add 1 ten thousand to 9 ten thousands to get 10 ten thousands.

> 10 ten thousands = 1 hundred thousand We write 1 hundred thousand as 100 000.

> 10 ten thousands = 1 hundred thousand

Hundred Thousands	Ten Thousands	Thousands	Hundreds	Tens	Ones
	⦾⦾⦾⦾⦾ ⦾⦾⦾⦾⦾				

⬇

Hundred Thousands	Ten Thousands	Thousands	Hundreds	Tens	Ones
●					
1	0	0	0	0	0
stands for 1 hundred thousand or 100 000	stands for 0 ten thousands or 0	stands for 0 thousands or 0	stands for 0 hundreds or 0	stands for 0 tens or 0	stands for 0 ones or 0

2 Count in steps of 100 000.

100 000	one hundred thousand
200 000	two hundred thousand
300 000	three hundred thousand
☐	four hundred thousand
☐	five hundred thousand
600 000	☐
700 000	☐
☐	eight hundred thousand
900 000	☐

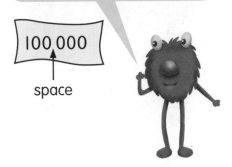

We leave a space between the thousands digit and the hundreds digit. This helps us to read the number easily.

100 000

space

3 What is the number in numerals and in words?

Hundred Thousands	Ten Thousands	Thousands	Hundreds	Tens	Ones
●●● ●●●	○○○ ○○	●● ●	●		●● ●●
stands for 6 hundred thousands	stands for 5 ten thousands	stands for 3 thousands	stands for 1 hundred	stands for 0 tens	stands for 4 ones

	In Numerals	In Words
6 hundred thousands	600 000	Six hundred thousand
5 ten thousands	50 000	Fifty thousand
3 thousands	3 000	Three thousand
1 hundred	100	One hundred
0 tens	0	
4 ones	4	Four

In numerals, the number is **653 104**.

In words, the number is **six hundred and fifty-three thousand, one hundred and four**.

4 **a** What is the number in numerals and in words?

Hundred Thousands	Ten Thousands	Thousands	Hundreds	Tens	Ones

stands for 5 hundred thousands / stands for 5 ten thousands / stands for 7 thousands / stands for 6 hundreds / stands for 7 tens / stands for 6 ones

	In Numerals	In Words
◻ hundred thousands	◻	◻
◻ ten thousands	◻	◻
◻ thousands	◻	◻
◻ hundreds	◻	◻
◻ tens	◻	◻
◻ ones	◻	◻

In numerals, the number is ◻.

In words, the number is ◻.

b What is the number in numerals and in words?

Hundred Thousands	Ten Thousands	Thousands	Hundreds	Tens	Ones

In numerals, the number is ◻.

In words, the number is ◻.

5 Read these numbers.

a

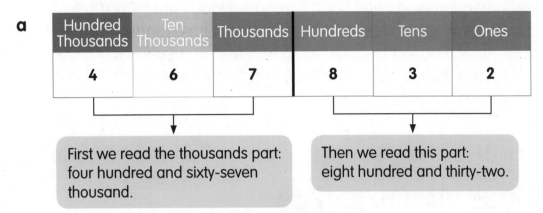

Hundred Thousands	Ten Thousands	Thousands	Hundreds	Tens	Ones
4	6	7	8	3	2

First we read the thousands part: four hundred and sixty-seven thousand.

Then we read this part: eight hundred and thirty-two.

467 832 is **four hundred and sixty-seven thousand, eight hundred and thirty-two**.

b   767 767

767 767 is **seven hundred and sixty-seven thousand, seven hundred and sixty-seven**.

6 Read these numbers.

a   325 176   **b**   438 834

c   906 096   **d**   555 555

e   680 806   **f**   700 007

Practice Book 5A, p. I

7 Count in hundred thousands.

1 hundred thousand (100 000), 2 hundred thousands (200 000),
3 hundred thousands (300 000), 4 hundred thousands (400 000),
5 hundred thousands (500 000), 6 hundred thousands (600 000),
7 hundred thousands (700 000), 8 hundred thousands (800 000),
9 hundred thousands (900 000), ⬭.

Add 1 hundred thousand to 9 hundred thousands to get 10 hundred thousands.

10 hundred thousands = 1 million
We write 1 million as 1 000 000.

1 thousand thousands = 1 million.

10 hundred thousands = 1 million

Millions	Hundred Thousands	Ten Thousands	Thousands	Hundreds	Tens	Ones
	●●●●● ●●●●●					

Millions	Hundred Thousands	Ten Thousands	Thousands	Hundreds	Tens	Ones
⬤						
1	0	0	0	0	0	0

stands for 1 million or 1 000 000	stands for 0 hundred thousands or 0	stands for 0 ten thousands or 0	stands for 0 thousands or 0	stands for 0 hundreds or 0	stands for 0 tens or 0	stands for 0 ones or 0

8 Count in steps of I 000 000.

I 000 000   one million

2 000 000   two million

3 000 000   three million

4 000 000   ☐

5 000 000   ☐

☐   six million

☐   seven million

8 000 000   ☐

☐   nine million

I0 000 000   ten million

I 000 000

first   second
space   space

We leave two spaces.
The first space helps us
to read the millions.
The second space helps us
to read the thousands.

9 This house costs more than £I 000 000.

Can you think of
other things that
cost millions of
pounds?

The population of Wales is more than 3 000 000.

According to the 20II census,
the population of Wales was
about 3 060 000.

10 What is the number in numerals and in words?

Millions	Hundred Thousands	Ten Thousands	Thousands	Hundreds	Tens	Ones
stands for 3 millions	stands for 5 hundred thousands	stands for 6 ten thousands	stands for 7 thousands	stands for 0 hundreds	stands for 4 tens	stands for 5 ones

	In Numerals	**In Words**
3 millions	3 000 000	Three million
5 hundred thousands	500 000	Five hundred thousand
6 ten thousands	60 000	Sixty thousand
7 thousands	7 000	Seven thousand
0 hundreds	0	
4 tens	40	Forty
5 ones	5	Five

In numerals, the number is **3 567 045**.

In words, the number is **three million, five hundred and sixty-seven thousand and forty-five**.

Activity

11 Work in groups.

Go to a news website and do a search for news articles containing the word 'millions'.
Print out the search results your group gets.
Discuss the use of 'millions' in the news articles with your class.

12 **a** What is the number in numerals and in words?

Millions	Hundred Thousands	Ten Thousands	Thousands	Hundreds	Tens	Ones
●● ●●	●●● ●●●		●●● ●●	●●●	●●● ●●● ●	●●● ●●● ●●●

| stands for 4 millions | stands for 6 hundred thousands | stands for 0 ten thousands | stands for 5 thousands | stands for 3 hundreds | stands for 7 tens | stands for 9 ones |

	In Numerals	In Words
▭ millions	▭	▭
▭ hundred thousands	▭	▭
▭ ten thousands	▭	
▭ thousands	▭	▭
▭ hundreds	▭	▭
▭ tens	▭	▭
▭ ones	▭	▭

In numerals, the number is ▭.

In words, the number is ▭.

b What is the number in numerals and in words?

Millions	Hundred Thousands	Ten Thousands	Thousands	Hundreds	Tens	Ones
●●● ●●●	●●●	●● ●●		●●● ●●	●●● ●●● ●●	●

In numerals, the number is ▭.

In words, the number is ▭.

13 Read these numbers.

a

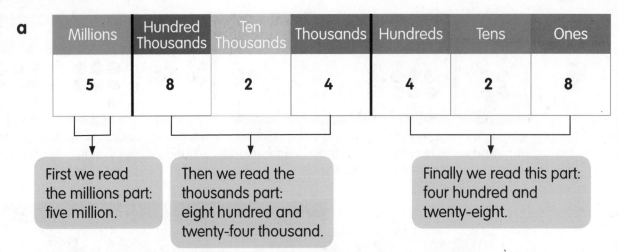

Millions	Hundred Thousands	Ten Thousands	Thousands	Hundreds	Tens	Ones
5	8	2	4	4	2	8

First we read the millions part: five million.

Then we read the thousands part: eight hundred and twenty-four thousand.

Finally we read this part: four hundred and twenty-eight.

5 824 428 is **five million, eight hundred and twenty-four thousand, four hundred and twenty-eight**.

b   6 035 350

6 035 350 is **six million, thirty-five thousand, three hundred and fifty**.

14 Read these numbers.

a   1 234 567   b   2 653 356

c   4 404 044   d   8 888 888

e   5 090 909   f   7 006 060

Home Maths

Explain that to read large numbers, your child only needs to know how to read up to three digits. For example, to read 9 375 608, they have to be able to read only 9 and 375 and 608. We say **million** after 9 and **thousand** after 375. This means 9 375 608 is read as nine **million**, three hundred and seventy-five **thousand**, six hundred and eight.

Activity

15 Work in pairs.

a Take turns to make a 6-digit number using the digits 5, 2, 0, 0, 0 and 0. Start with the digit 2 or 5, for example, 500 200. Then tell your partner the first digit of your number. Your partner will try to guess your number. Each time they guess, they should write the number in numerals and in words. They score I point if they guess the number correctly within three tries.

b Turn your calculator on.

To display the number 3 210 456 on your calculator, press
③, ②, ①, ⓪, ④, ⑤, ⑥ in order.
To clear the display on your calculator, press ⓒ.
Take turns to type in a 6-digit or 7-digit number on your calculator and ask your partner to read the number.
Remember to press ⓒ before you type in a new number.

Let's Practise!

16 Write in numerals.

a Two hundred thousand, one hundred and six.
b Six hundred and seventy-three thousand, nine hundred and eleven.
c Five hundred and eighteen thousand and four.
d Seven million, three hundred and thirteen thousand.
e Nine million, five hundred and twenty.
f Five million, two thousand and twelve.

17 Write in words.

a 215 905	**b** 819 002	**c** 120 040
d 6 430 000	**e** 5 009 300	**f** 9 722 830

Practice Book 5A, p. 5

Let's Learn!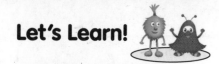

Place and value

I

Hundred Thousands	Ten Thousands	Thousands	Hundreds	Tens	Ones
8	6	I	2	5	7

In **861 257**:

the digit 8 stands for **800 000**
the **value** of the digit 8 is **800 000**

the digit 6 stands for **60 000**
the **value** of the digit 6 is **60 000**

the digit I stands for **1000**
the **value** of the digit I is **1000**.

2 In **861 257**:

the digit 8 is in the **hundred thousands** place
the digit 6 is in the **ten thousands** place
the digit I is in the **thousands** place.

3 Answer these questions.

a In 670 932, the value of the digit **6** is [____].

b What is the value of the digit **2** in each of the following 6-digit numbers?

   i   812 679   **ii**   260 153   **iii**   827 917

4 Answer these questions.

a In 937 016, the digit ⬚ is in the hundreds place.

b In 124 573, the digit in the hundred thousands place is ⬚.

c In 971 465, the digit 6 is in the ⬚ place.

d In 289 219, the digit 8 is in the ⬚ place.

e In what place is the digit **2** in each of the following numbers?

 i 18**2** 679 ii **2**60 153 iii 8**2**7 917

5

Look at the values of the digits in 381 492.
For example, the value of the digit 3 is 300 000.
We can add the values of the digits to get the number.

381 492 = 300 000 + 80 000 + 1000 + 400 + 90 + 2
        = 381 000 + 492

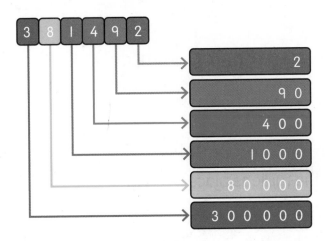

6 Answer these questions.

a 761 902 = 700 000 + ⬚ + 1000 + 900 + 2

b 124 003 = ⬚ + 3

c 900 356 = 900 000 + 300 + ⬚ + 6

d 368 215 = ⬚ + 8000 + 200 + 15

7

Millions	Hundred Thousands	Ten Thousands	Thousands	Hundreds	Tens	Ones
I	6	4	9	0	0	0

In **I 649 000**:

the digit I stands for **I 000 000**
the value of the digit I is ◯

the digit 6 stands for **600 000**
the value of the digit 6 is ◯

the digit 4 is in the **ten thousands** place

the digit 9 is in the ◯ place.

8

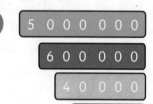

$5\,649\,000 = 5\,000\,000$
$+ 600\,000 + 40\,000 + 9000$

or

$5\,649\,000 = 5\,000\,000 + 649\,000$

9 Answer these questions.

a In 7 296 000:

   i the digit ◯ is in the millions place

   ii the value of the digit 6 is ◯

   iii the digit 2 stands for ◯

   iv the digit 9 is in the ◯ place.

b $7\,200\,000 = 7\,000\,000 +$ ◯

c $6\,235\,000 =$ ◯ $+ 235\,000$

d $2\,459\,000 = 2\,000\,000 + 400\,000 +$ ◯ $+ 9000$

Activity

10 Work in pairs. Write down a 6-digit or a 7-digit number.
Give clues for your partner to guess your number.
For example, if you wrote down 359100, you can say:

> My number has six digits.
> The digit 5 is next to the digit 3, which has a value of 300000.
> The digit 9 is in the thousands place.
> The value of the digit in the hundreds place is 100.
> There are two zeros in my number.
> What is my number?

Take turns to guess each other's numbers.

Let's Practise!

11 What is the value of the digit **5** in each of the following numbers?

    a   64 0**5**1   **b**   783 **5**62   **c**   1**5**7 300   **d**   **5**91 368

12 In the number 357 921, the value of the digit 3 is ⬚
and the digit 7 is in the ⬚ place.

13   829 359 = 800 000 + ⬚ + 300 + 50 + 9

14 What is the value of the digit **6** in each of the following numbers?

    a   **6** 390 000   **b**   8 100 **6**00   **c**   7 **6**20 548

15 Answer these questions.

    a   In 7 005 000, the digit ⬚ is in the millions place.

    b   In 2 321 654, the digit in the hundred thousands place is ⬚.

16 **a**   2 403 800 = ⬚ + 400 000 + 3000 + 800

    b   9 197 328 = 9 000 000 + 197 000 + ⬚

Practice Book 5A, p. 7

Let's Learn!

Comparing numbers within 10 million

1

When we compare numbers, we look at the value of each digit starting from the left.

Which number is smaller: 237 981 or 500 600?

Hundred Thousands	Ten Thousands	Thousands	Hundreds	Tens	Ones
2	3	7	9	8	1
5	0	0	6	0	0

Compare the values of the digits starting from the left.
2 hundred thousands is smaller than 5 hundred thousands.
So 237 981 is smaller than 500 600.

2 Which number is greater: 712 935 or 712 846?

Hundred Thousands	Ten Thousands	Thousands	Hundreds	Tens	Ones
7	1	2	9	3	5
7	1	2	8	4	6

Compare the values of the digits starting from the left.
If they are the same, continue to compare until the values of the digits are not the same.
Here the values of the digits in the hundreds place are not the same.

[ ] is greater than [ ].

So 712 935 is [ ] than 712 846.

3 Which number is smaller: 3 506 017 or 5 306 007?

Millions	Hundred Thousands	Ten Thousands	Thousands	Hundreds	Tens	Ones
3	5	0	6	0	I	7
5	3	0	6	0	0	7

Compare the values of the digits starting from the left.
3 millions is smaller than 5 millions.
So 3 506 017 is smaller than 5 306 007.

4 Which number is greater: 4 730 589 or 4 703 985?
4 **73**0 589
4 **70**3 985

Compare the values of the digits starting from the left.
Here the values of the digits in the ten thousands place are different.

Compare the values of the digits in the ten thousands place.

[ ] is greater than [ ].

So [ ] is greater than [ ].

5 Which number is greater? Which is smaller?
Use **greater than** or **smaller than**.

a   345 932 is [ ] 435 990.

b   100 400 is [ ] 99 900.

c   220 000 is [ ] 219 099.

d   5 245 721 is [>] 524 572.

e   3 143 820 is [ ] 4 134 820.

f   6 680 910 is [ ] 668 091.

6 Arrange the numbers in order, beginning with the smallest.

   a   324 688, 32 468, 3 246 880

   b   1 600 456, 1 604 654, 1 064 645

7 What is the next number in each pattern?

   a   231 590, 331 590, 431 590, 531 590, …

       331 590 is 100 000 more than **2**31 590.
       431 590 is 100 000 more than **3**31 590.
       531 590 is 100 000 more than **4**31 590.

       100 000 more than **5**31 590 is **6**31 590.
       The next number is 631 590.

   b   755 482, 705 482, 655 482, 605 482, …

       705 482 is 50 000 less than **75**5 482.
       655 482 is 50 000 less than **70**5 482.
       605 482 is 50 000 less than **65**5 482.

       50 000 less than **60**5 482 is **55**5 482.
       The next number is 555 482.

8 What is the next number in each pattern?

   a   1 345 024, 3 345 024, 5 345 024, …

       3 345 024 is ☐ more than **1** 345 024.

       5 345 024 is ☐ more than **3** 345 024.

       ☐ more than 5 345 024 is ☐.
       The next number is ☐.

   b   820 346, 810 346, 800 346, …

       810 346 is ☐ less than 820 346.

       800 346 is ☐ less than 810 346.

       ☐ less than 800 346 is ☐.
       The next number is ☐.

Let's Practise!

9 **a** Which is greater: 568 912 or 568 921?

b Which is smaller: 71 690 or 100 345?

10 **a** Which is the greatest: 81 630, 81 603 or 816 300?

b Which is the smallest: 125 000, 12 500 or 25 000?

11 Arrange the following numbers in order, beginning with the smallest.
901 736, 714 800, 199 981

12 Arrange the following numbers in order, beginning with the greatest.
36 925, 925 360, 360 925

13 Complete this number pattern. Give the rule for the pattern.
325 410, ⬜, 305 410, 295 410, ⬜, 275 410

14 Complete this number pattern. Give the rule for the pattern.
2 390 000, 3 400 000, 4 410 000, ⬜, 6 430 000

15 What is the next number in each pattern?

a 580 356, 600 356, 620 356, 640 356, …

600 356 is ⬜ more than 580 356.

620 356 is ⬜ more than 600 356.

640 356 is ⬜ more than 620 356.

⬜ more than 640 356 is ⬜.

b 4 030 875, 3 830 875, 3 630 875, 3 430 875, …

⬜ less than 3 430 875 is ⬜.

> Practice Book 5A, p. 11

Let's Learn!

Rounding to the nearest thousand and estimating

We round numbers so that we are able to estimate.

I have £432. Noogol has £920. We need £2000 to buy a computer. How much more money do we need?

Zoogol has about £400. I have about £900. We have about £1300 altogether. We need about £700 more to buy the computer.

I Let's recall rounding to the nearest hundred.

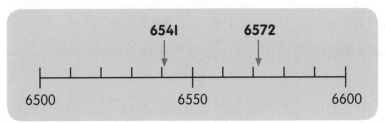

6541 is between 6500 and 6600.
6541 is nearer to 6500 than to 6600.
6541 is **6500** when rounded to the nearest hundred.

6572 is between 6500 and 6600.
6572 is nearer to 6600 than to 6500.
6572 is **6600** when rounded to the nearest hundred.

We say 6541 is approximately equal to **6500** and
6572 is approximately equal to **6600**.

We write 6541 ≈ **6500**
6572 ≈ **6600**

We use the approximation sign (≈) to stand for **approximately equal to**. It shows what the numbers are rounded to.

2 **a**

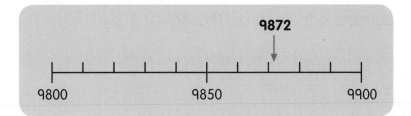

9872 is between 9800 and ⬭.

9872 is nearer to ⬭ than ⬭.

9872 is ⬭ when rounded to the nearest hundred.

9872 ≈ ⬭

b   What is 8137 rounded to the nearest hundred? ⬭

3   Let's round to the nearest thousand.
What is 6541 rounded to the nearest thousand?

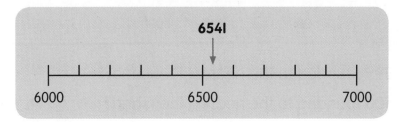

6541 is between 6000 and 7000.
6541 is nearer to 7000 than to 6000.
6541 is **7000** when rounded to the nearest thousand.
6541 ≈ 7000

4   What is 8276 rounded to the nearest thousand?

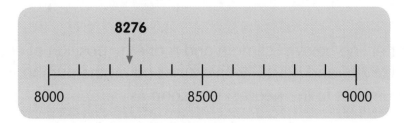

8276 is between 8000 and 9000.
8276 is nearer to 8000 than 9000.
8276 is **8000** when rounded to the nearest thousand.
8276 ≈ ⬭

5 What is 9500 rounded to the nearest thousand?

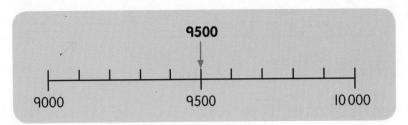

9500 is exactly halfway between 9000 and 10 000.
In this case, we round 9500 to 10 000.
So 9500 is **10 000** when rounded to the nearest thousand.
9500 ≈ 10 000

6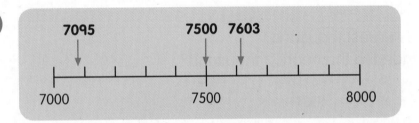

a   What is 7095 rounded to the nearest thousand?

b   What is 7500 rounded to the nearest thousand?

c   What is 7603 rounded to the nearest thousand?

7 Round 85 210 to the nearest thousand.

The number is between 85 000 and 86 000.
85 210 is nearer to 85 000 than to 86 000.
85 210 is 85 000 when rounded to the nearest thousand.
85 210 ≈ 85 000

8 Copy the number line below. Estimate and mark the position of each of the numbers, 125 780 and 125 231 with a cross (✗) on the number line. Round these numbers to the nearest thousand.

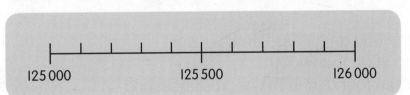

9 Round these numbers to the nearest thousand.

a   6321   b   6509

c   1098   d   9873

e   6995   f   12051

g   65500   h   89773

i   325699   j   600039

10 Round these numbers to the nearest thousand.

6521 ≈ 7000
5079 ≈ 5000

Then estimate the value of: **a**   6521 + 5079   **b**   6521 − 5079

a   6521 + 5079 ≈ 7000 + 5000
                = 12000

> There is a change in sign because we are not approximating the sum of 7000 and 5000. This is the actual sum of the two rounded numbers.

b   6521 − 5079 ≈ 7000 − ⬚
                = ⬚

11 Round the numbers to the nearest thousand. Then estimate the value of:

a   7192 + 1642

b   5701 − 3214

c   6290 + 5500 + 3719

d   9810 − 1600 − 7391

12 Estimate the value of 7120 × 5.

First round 7120 to the nearest thousand.

$7120 \approx 7000$

$7120 \times 5 \approx 7000 \times 5$
$= 35\,000$

13 Estimate the value of 6327 × 7.

Round the 4-digit number to the nearest thousand first.

$6327 \times 7 \approx \boxed{} \times 7$

$= \boxed{}$

14 Round the 4-digit number to the nearest thousand. Then estimate the value of:

a   2145 × 7   b   8756 × 6   c   2632 × 8

d   4979 × 5   e   9218 × 4   f   6380 × 9

15 Estimate the value of 3465 ÷ 6.

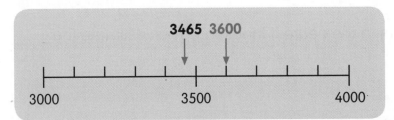

To estimate 3465 ÷ 6, we choose a number close to 3465 that can be divided by 6 exactly.

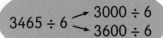

$3465 \div 6 \begin{cases} 3000 \div 6 \\ 3600 \div 6 \end{cases}$

3465 is closer to 3600 than 3000.

So $3465 \div 6 \approx 3600 \div 6 = 600$.

16 Estimate the value of 6742 ÷ 8.

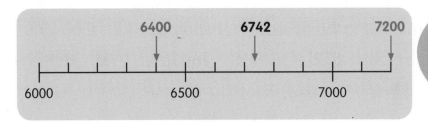

6400   **6742**   7200

6000   6500   7000

6742 ÷ 8 ↗ 6400 ÷ 8
         ↘ 7200 ÷ 8

6742 is nearer to
6400 than to 7200.

So 6742 ÷ 8 ≈ ⬚ ÷ 8 = ⬚.

Activity

17 Work in pairs.
A house has 3 bedrooms, a living room,
a dining room, a bathroom and a kitchen.
The new owners want to renovate the
house. Estimate how much they would
need to spend on the renovation by first
rounding each cost to the nearest
thousand pounds.

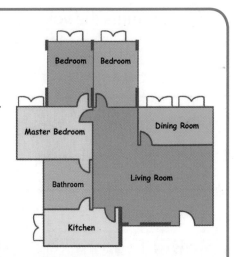

Description	Cost
Oak flooring for the living room, dining room and 3 bedrooms	£7650 per room
Bookshelves in 2 rooms	£3840 per room
Cupboards in master bedroom	£4621
New kitchen	£7705
Other furniture	£16 500

Let's Practise!

18 Round each number to the nearest: **i** hundred **ii** thousand.

    a 7005   **b** 8321   **c** 7603   **d** 8997

19 Round the 4-digit numbers to the nearest thousand. Then estimate the value of:

    a 3471 + 4207   **b** 3670 − 2189

    c 9246 − 2355 − 1478   **d** 3322 × 8

20 Estimate the value of:

    a 1745 ÷ 3   **b** 2343 ÷ 4

    c 4467 ÷ 6   **d** 4219 ÷ 5

    e 6581 ÷ 7   **f** 8502 ÷ 9

Practice Book 5A, p. 15

Maths Journal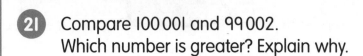

21 Compare 100 001 and 99 002.
Which number is greater? Explain why.

22 Round **a** 763 to the nearest hundred

           b 3730 to the nearest thousand.

Ella rounded 763 to 700 and 3730 to 3000.
Explain the mistakes she made.

Let's Wrap It Up!

You have learnt to:

- count in ten thousands and hundred thousands
- read and write numbers up to 10 million in words and numerals
- identify the place and value of each digit of a number up to 10 million
- compare numbers within 10 million
- complete number patterns by adding or subtracting
- round numbers to the nearest thousand
- estimate sums, differences, products and quotients.

Let's Revise!

The land area of some countries are shown below.

Country	Land Area in km²
Canada	9 976 140
France	547 030
Hong Kong	1092
Indonesia	1 919 440
Maldives	300
Singapore	693
Belgium	30 280
Thailand	514 000

a Write the value of the land area of Canada in words.

Nine million, nine hundred and seventy-six thousand, one hundred and forty.

b Which country has the smallest land area? What is its land area in numerals?

Maldives has a land area of 300 km².

Let's Wrap It Up!

c Arrange the countries in order, beginning with the country with the greatest land area.
Canada, Indonesia, France, Thailand, Belgium, Hong Kong, Singapore and Maldives.

d Which countries have a land area of more than $1\,000\,000$ km²?
Canada and Indonesia.

e Which country has a larger land area, France or Thailand?
France has a larger land area than Thailand.

f Which countries have a land area of 1000 km² when rounded to the nearest thousand?
Singapore and Hong Kong.

Put On Your Thinking Caps!

23 Three cards have different whole numbers on them.
Each number equals 30 when rounded to the nearest ten.

?　?　?

a What are the smallest and greatest possible numbers?

b What can the three numbers be?

24 Without adding the 99s together, use a quicker way to find the value of:
a $99 + 99$
b $99 + 99 + 99 + 99 + 99 + 99$
What is the value of the digit in the ones place in each case?
c What is the least number of 99s which must be added to get a I in the ones place?

Practice Book 5A, p. 2I　　Practice Book 5A, p. 22

Whole Numbers (2)

Let's Learn!

Using a calculator

Get to know your calculator

I Follow the steps to type in numbers on your calculator.

Turn your calculator on.
To type in 12 345, press: [1] [2] [3] [4] [5]
To clear the display on your calculator, press: [C]

	Display
	0
	12345
	0

Activity

2 Work in pairs.

Type in these numbers on your calculator. Clear the display on your calculator before typing in the next number.

a 735 **b** 9038 **c** 23 104 **d** 505 602

Check the numbers displayed on your calculator with those on your partner's calculator.
Do you both get the same numbers on the display screen?

Addition

3 a Add 417 and 9086.

Press	Display
[C]	0
[4] [1] [7]	417
[+] [9] [0] [8] [6]	9086
[=]	9503

The sum is 9503.

b Find the sum of £1275 and £876.

Remember to write the correct unit in your answer.

Press	Display
C	0
1 2 7 5	1275
+ 8 7 6	876
=	2151

The sum of £1275 and £876 is £2151.

Subtraction

4 **a** Subtract 6959 from 17358.

Press	Display
C	0
1 7 3 5 8	17358
– 6 9 5 9	6959
=	10399

The answer is 10399.

b Find the difference between 1005 kg and 248 kg.

Remember to write **kg** in your answer.

Press	Display
C	0
1 0 0 5	1005
– 2 4 8	248
=	757

The difference between 1005 kg and 248 kg is 757 kg.

Activity

5

Remember to press C before you start working on each question.

Work in pairs to answer these questions:

a   7064 + 2378   **b**   10 213 + 897

c   3675 – 1976   **d**   12 310 – 9342

e   734 km + 9868 km   **f**   £3250 – £1865

Think of one addition and one subtraction sentence.
Ask your partner to work them out using a calculator. Use your calculator to check whether your partner's answers are correct.

Multiplication

6   **a**   Multiply 253 by 127.

Press	Display
C	0
2 5 3	253
× 1 2 7	127
=	32 131

The answer is 32 131.

b   Find the area of a rectangle with a length of 36 cm and a width of 24 cm.

Area = Length × Width
Remember that the unit for area is cm², m², etc.

Press	Display
C	0
3 6	36
× 2 4	24
=	864

The area of the rectangle is 864 cm².

Division

7 **a** Divide 4572 by 36.

Press	Display
C	0
4 5 7 2	4572
÷ 3 6	36
=	127

The answer is 127.

b What is 168 ℓ divided by 16?

Press	Display
C	0
1 6 8	168
÷ 1 6	16
=	10.5

168 ℓ divided by 16 is 10·5 ℓ.

Activity

8 Work in pairs to answer these questions:

Remember to press C before you start working on each question.

a 1065 × 97   **b** 13 674 × 7   **c** 1075 ÷ 25

d 10 840 ÷ 40   **e** 25 m × 48 m   **f** 406 g ÷ 28

Think of one multiplication and one division sentence. Ask your partner to work them out using a calculator. Use your calculator to check whether your partner's answers are correct.

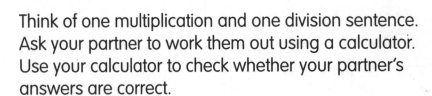

Practice Book 5A, p.23

Let's Learn!

Multiplying by tens, hundreds or thousands

Multiplying by 10

1 | 10 | 10 | 10 | 10 | 10 | 10 | 10 |

$7 \times 10 = 70$

| 10 | 10 | 10 | 10 | 10 | 10 | 10 | 10 | 10 |

$9 \times 10 = 90$

| 10 | 10 | 10 | 10 | 10 | 10 | 10 | 10 | 10 | 10 |

$10 \times 10 = 100$

| 10 | 10 | 10 | 10 | 10 | 10 | 10 | 10 | 10 | 10 | 10 | 10 |

$12 \times 10 = 120$

Look at the chart below.

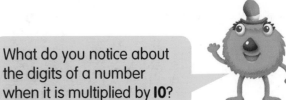

$7 \times 10 = 7$ tens
$= 70$

$9 \times 10 = 9$ tens
$= 90$

$10 \times 10 = 10$ tens
$= 100$

$12 \times 10 = 12$ tens
$= 120$

	Hundreds	Tens	Ones
7			7
7 × 10		7	0
9			9
9 × 10		9	0
10		1	0
10 × 10	1	0	0
12		1	2
12 × 10	1	2	0

What do you notice about the digits of a number when it is multiplied by **10**?

You can see in the chart that each digit moves **one** place to the **left**.

33

Activity

2 Copy the chart below.

	Hundred Thousands	Ten Thousands	Thousands	Hundreds	Tens	Ones
231				2	3	1
231 × 10			2	3	1	0
2345			2	3	4	5
2345 × 10						
4108			4	1	0	8
4108 × 10						

Complete the chart and write down the value of:

a 231 × 10 **b** 2345 × 10 **c** 4108 × 10

3 Find the value of:

a 60 × 10 **b** 135 × 10 **c** 503 × 10
d 2876 × 10 **e** 6082 × 10 **f** 6210 × 10

When a **whole number** is multiplied by **10**, what is a quick way to get the answer?

4 Find the missing numbers.

a 8 × ⬚ = 80 **b** 22 × ⬚ = 220
c ⬚ × 10 = 5280 **d** ⬚ × 10 = 74 600

Multiplying by tens

5 6 × 20

20	20	20	20	20	20

10	10	10	10	10	10	10	10	10	10	10	10

6 × 20 = 6 × 2 tens
= 6 × 2 × 10
= 12 × 10
= 120

Multiplying a number by 20 is the same as multiplying it by 2 and then by 10.

27 × 30 = 27 × 3 tens
= 27 × 3 × 10
= 81 × 10
= 810

Activity

6 Copy this table and complete it by multiplying each number by 6 and by 60. An example is shown.

	× 6	× 60
42	252	2520
65		
861		

Look at the answers in the table. What are the missing numbers?

a   42 × 60 = 42 × 6 × ⬚

b   65 × 60 = 65 × ⬚ × ⬚

c   861 × 60 = 861 × ⬚ × ⬚

7 Find the missing numbers.

a   62 × 40 = 62 × 4 × 10
= ⬚ × 10
= ⬚

b   307 × 80 = 307 × ⬚ × 10
= ⬚ × 10
= ⬚

Home Maths

Show your child how they can use their calculator to check that:
723 × 30 = 723 × 10 × 3 = 723 × 3 × 10.

8 Find the value of:

a 31×60

b 274×50

c 1970×90

d 8145×40

Multiplying by 100 or 1000

9

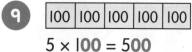

$5 \times 100 = 500$

$12 \times 100 = 1200$

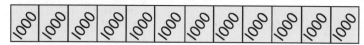

$5 \times 1000 = 5000$

$12 \times 1000 = 12\,000$

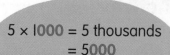

$5 \times 100 = 5 \text{ hundreds}$
$\qquad = 500$

$12 \times 100 = 12 \text{ hundreds}$
$\qquad = 1200$

$5 \times 1000 = 5 \text{ thousands}$
$\qquad = 5000$

$12 \times 1000 = 12 \text{ thousands}$
$\qquad = 12\,000$

Look at the chart below.

	Ten Thousands	Thousands	Hundreds	Tens	Ones
5					5
5 × 100			5	0	0
12				1	2
12 × 100		1	2	0	0
5					5
5 × 1000		5	0	0	0
12				1	2
12 × 1000	1	2	0	0	0

What do you notice about the digits of a number when it is multiplied by **100** and by **1000**?

Activity

10 Copy the chart below.

	Millions	Hundred Thousands	Ten Thousands	Thousands	Hundreds	Tens	Ones
174					1	7	4
174 × 100			1	7	4	0	0
174 × 1000		1	7	4	0	0	0
3298				3	2	9	8
3298 × 100							
3298 × 1000							

Complete the chart and write down the value of:

a 174 × 100   **b** 174 × 1000

c 3298 × 100   **d** 3298 × 1000

When a **whole number** is multiplied by **100**, what is a quick way to get the answer?

When a **whole number** is multiplied by **1000**, what is a quick way to get the answer?

11 Find the value of:

a 27 × 100   **b** 615 × 100   **c** 9670 × 100

d 18 × 1000   **e** 487 × 1000   **f** 5346 × 1000

12 Find the missing numbers.

a 26 × ☐ = 2600   **b** 195 × ☐ = 195 000

c ☐ × 100 = 49 000   **d** ☐ × 1000 = 168 000

Multiplying by hundreds or thousands

13 7 × 200

200	200	200	200	200	200	200

100	100	100	100	100	100	100	100	100	100	100	100	100	100

$$7 \times 200 = 7 \times 2 \text{ hundreds}$$
$$= 7 \times 2 \times 100$$
$$= 14 \times 100$$
$$= 1400$$

> Multiplying a number by 200 is the same as multiplying it by 2 and then by 100.

$$93 \times 300 = 93 \times 3 \text{ hundreds}$$
$$= 93 \times 3 \times 100$$
$$= 279 \times 100$$
$$= 27\,900$$

Activity

14 Copy this table and complete it by multiplying each number by 7 and by 700. An example is shown.

	× 7	× 700
78	546	54 600
113		
251		

Look at the answers in the table. What are the missing numbers?

a 78 × 700 = 78 × 7 × ▢

b 113 × 700 = 113 × ▢ × ▢

c 251 × 700 = 251 × ▢ × ▢

15 Find the missing numbers.

a 72 × 400 = 72 × 4 × 100
= ▢ × 100
= ▢

b 123 × 700 = 123 × ▢ × ▢
= ▢ × 100
= ▢

16 Find the value of:

a 81 × 500

b 932 × 800

c 6455 × 900

d 6007 × 800

17 5 × 3000

3000	3000	3000	3000	3000
1000 1000 1000	1000 1000 1000	1000 1000 1000	1000 1000 1000	1000 1000 1000

5 × 3000 = 5 × 3 thousands
       = 5 × 3 × 1000
       = 15 × 1000
       = 15 000

Multiplying a number by 3000 is the same as multiplying it by 3 and then by 1000.

67 × 5000 = 67 × 5 thousands
        = 67 × 5 × 1000
        = 335 × 1000
        = 335 000

Activity

18 Copy this table and complete it by multiplying each number by 7 and by 7000. An example is shown.

	× 7	× 7000
56	392	392 000
203		
412		

Look at the answers in the table. What are the missing numbers?

a 56 × 7000 = 56 × 7 × ☐

b 203 × 7000 = 203 × ☐ × ☐

c 412 × 7000 = 412 × ☐ × ☐

19 Find the missing numbers.

a $6 \times 5000 = 6 \times 5 \times 1000$

$= \boxed{} \times 1000$

$= \boxed{}$

b $18 \times 6000 = 18 \times \boxed{} \times \boxed{}$

$= \boxed{} \times 1000$

$= \boxed{}$

20 Find the value of:

a 73×4000

b 905×8000

c 654×3000

d 807×9000

21 Estimate the value of 632×26.

$632 \times 26 \approx 600 \times 30$

$= 600 \times 3 \times 10$

$= 1800 \times 10$

$= 18\,000$

> Round 632 to the nearest hundred.
> $632 \approx 600$
> Round 26 to the nearest ten.
> $26 \approx 30$
> $632 \times 26 = 16\,432$
> $18\,000$ is a reasonable estimate.

22 Estimate the value of 128×57.

$128 \approx \boxed{}$ $\qquad$ $57 \approx 60$

So $128 \times 57 \approx \boxed{} \times 60$

$= \boxed{} \times 6 \times 10$

$= \boxed{} \times 10$

$= \boxed{}$

> Even if you have a calculator, it is important to use estimation to check that your answers are reasonable.

23 Estimate.

a 702×15

b 38×246

c 511×62

24 Kerry sold 1215 packets of plastic spoons at her shop. There were 26 spoons in each packet. Estimate the number of spoons she sold.

$1215 \times 26 \approx 1000 \times 30$
$\qquad = 1000 \times 3 \times 10$
$\qquad = 3000 \times 10$
$\qquad = 30\,000$

She sold about 30 000 spoons.

Round 1215 to the nearest thousand.
$1215 \approx 1000$
Round 26 to the nearest ten.
$26 \approx 30$
$1215 \times 26 = 31\,590$
30 000 is a reasonable estimate.

25 Estimate the value of 1238 × 56.
$1238 \times 56 \approx 1000 \times \boxed{}$
$\qquad = 1000 \times \boxed{} \times \boxed{}$
$\qquad = \boxed{} \times \boxed{}$
$\qquad = \boxed{}$

26 Estimate.
  a   99 × 38   **b**   67 × 439
  c   9281 × 32   **d**   2065 × 41

Let's Practise!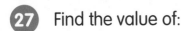

27 Find the value of:
  a   412 × 10   **b**   792 × 100   **c**   740 × 1000

28 Find the value of:
  a   703 × 60   **b**   815 × 700   **c**   169 × 3000

29 A machine in a factory produced 452 beads in a minute. Estimate the number of beads it would produce in 56 minutes.

30   Use your calculator to work out the following:
  a   3711 × 9   **b**   2087 × 37   **c**   1985 × 302

Use estimation to check if your answers are reasonable.

Practice Book 5A, p.25

Let's Learn!

Dividing by tens, hundreds or thousands

Dividing by 10

1

70

| 7 | 7 | 7 | 7 | 7 | 7 | 7 | 7 | 7 | 7 |

$70 \div 10 = 7$

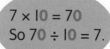
7 × 10 = 70
So 70 ÷ 10 = 7.

160

| 16 | 16 | 16 | 16 | 16 | 16 | 16 | 16 | 16 | 16 |

$160 \div 10 = 16$

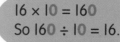
16 × 10 = 160
So 160 ÷ 10 = 16.

1800

| 180 | 180 | 180 | 180 | 180 | 180 | 180 | 180 | 180 | 180 |

$1800 \div 10 = 180$

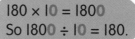
180 × 10 = 1800
So 1800 ÷ 10 = 180.

Look at the chart below.

	Thousands	Hundreds	Tens	Ones	•	Tenths
70			7	0		
70 ÷ 10				7		0
160		1	6	0		
160 ÷ 10			1	6		0
1800	1	8	0	0		
1800 ÷ 10		1	8	0		0

7·0 is 7.
16·0 is 16.
180·0 is 180.

What do you notice about the digits of a number when it is divided by **10**?

Activity

2 Copy the chart below.

	Thousands	Hundreds	Tens	Ones	•	Tenths
360		3	6	0		
360 ÷ 10			3	6		0
1580	1	5	8	0		
1580 ÷ 10						

Complete the chart and write down the value of:

When a **whole number** with **0** in the **ones place** is divided by **10**, what is a quick way to get the answer?

a   360 ÷ 10   **b**   1580 ÷ 10

3 Find the value of:

a   90 ÷ 10   **b**   380 ÷ 10   **c**   1900 ÷ 10

d   43 650 ÷ 10   **e**   23 040 ÷ 10   **f**   53 600 ÷ 10

4 Find the missing numbers.

a   2600 ÷ ⬚ = 260   **b**   19 500 ÷ ⬚ = 1950

c   ⬚ ÷ 10 = 4900   **d**   ⬚ ÷ 10 = 1680

Dividing by tens

5   60 ÷ 30 = 60 ÷ 10 ÷ 3
              = 6 ÷ 3
              = 2

Dividing by 30 is the same as dividing by 10 and then by 3.

420 ÷ 70 = 420 ÷ 10 ÷ 7
              = 42 ÷ 7
              = 6

Home Maths
Show your child how they can use their calculator to check that:
420 ÷ 70 = 420 ÷ 10 ÷ 7 = 420 ÷ 7 ÷ 10.

Activity

6 Copy this table and complete it by dividing each number by 10 and by 90. An example is shown.

	÷ 10	÷ 90
540	54	6
720		
810		

Look at the answers in the table. What are the missing numbers?

a $540 \div 90 = 540 \div 10 \div \boxed{}$ **b** $720 \div 90 = 720 \div \boxed{} \div \boxed{}$

c $810 \div 90 = 810 \div \boxed{} \div \boxed{}$

7 Find the missing numbers.

a $850 \div 50 = 850 \div 10 \div 5$
$\quad = \boxed{} \div 5$
$\quad = \boxed{}$

b $7200 \div 80 = 7200 \div \boxed{} \div \boxed{}$
$\quad = \boxed{} \div 8$
$\quad = \boxed{}$

8 Find the value of:

a $160 \div 40$ **b** $700 \div 50$

c $6320 \div 20$ **d** $8400 \div 60$

Dividing by 100 or 1000

9 $9 \times 100 = 900$
So $900 \div 100 = 9$.

$14 \times 100 = 1400$
So $1400 \div 100 = 14$.

$9 \times 1000 = 9000$
So $9000 \div 1000 = 9$.

$14 \times 1000 = 14\,000$
So $14\,000 \div 1000 = 14$.

10 Look at the chart below.

	Ten Thousands	Thousands	Hundreds	Tens	Ones •	Tenths	Hundredths	Thousandths
900			9	0	0			
900 ÷ 100					9	0	0	
1400		1	4	0	0			
1400 ÷ 100				1	4	0	0	
9000		9	0	0	0			
9000 ÷ 1000					9	0	0	0
14 000	1	4	0	0	0			
14 000 ÷ 1000				1	4	0	0	0

What do you notice about the digits of a number when it is divided by **100** and by **1000**?

9·00 is 9.
14·00 is 14.

9·000 is also 9.
14·000 is also 14.

Activity

11 Copy the chart below.

	Ten Thousands	Thousands	Hundreds	Tens	Ones	•	Tenths	Hundredths	Thousandths
700			7	0	0				
700 ÷ 100					7		0	0	
3600		3	6	0	0				
3600 ÷ 100									
8000		8	0	0	0				
8000 ÷ 1000									
54 000	5	4	0	0	0				
54 000 ÷ 1000									

Complete the chart and write down the value of:

a   700 ÷ 100   **b**   3600 ÷ 100

c   8000 ÷ 1000   **d**   54 000 ÷ 1000

When a **whole number with two zeros** as the last two digits is divided by **100**, what is a quick way to get the answer?

When a **whole number with three zeros** as the last three digits is divided by **1000**, what is a quick way to get the answer?

12 Find the value of:

a   400 ÷ 100   **b**   1500 ÷ 100   **c**   20 500 ÷ 100

d   10 000 ÷ 1000   **e**   124 000 ÷ 1000   **f**   3 230 000 ÷ 1000

Dividing by hundreds or thousands

13   600 ÷ 300 = 600 ÷ 100 ÷ 3
                        = 6 ÷ 3
                        = 2

Dividing a number by 300 is the same as dividing it by 100 and then by 3.

Dividing a number by 2000 is the same as dividing it by 1000 and then by 2.

6000 ÷ 2000 = 6000 ÷ 1000 ÷ 2
                        = 6 ÷ 2
                        = 3

Activity

14 Copy this table and complete it by dividing each number by 100 and by 600. An example is shown.

	÷ 100	÷ 600
1200	12	2
4200		
5400		

Look at the answers in the table. What are the missing numbers?

a 1200 ÷ 600 = 1200 ÷ 100 ÷ ⬚

b 4200 ÷ 600 = 4200 ÷ ⬚ ÷ ⬚

c 5400 ÷ 600 = 5400 ÷ ⬚ ÷ ⬚

15 Copy this table and complete it by dividing each number by 1000 and by 8000. An example is shown.

	÷ 1000	÷ 8000
32 000	32	4
48 000		
64 000		

Look at the answers in the table. What are the missing numbers?

a 32 000 ÷ 8000 = 32 000 ÷ 1000 ÷ ⬚

b 48 000 ÷ 8000 = 48 000 ÷ ⬚ ÷ ⬚

c 64 000 ÷ 8000 = 64 000 ÷ ⬚ ÷ ⬚

16 Find the missing numbers.

a 2400 ÷ 400 = 2400 ÷ 100 ÷ 4   b 35 000 ÷ 7000 = 35 000 ÷ 1000 ÷ 7

= ⬚ ÷ 4   = ⬚ ÷ 7

= ⬚   = ⬚

Encourage your child to use their calculator to check that:
2400 ÷ 400 = 2400 ÷ 100 ÷ 4 and 35 000 ÷ 7000 = 35 000 ÷ 1000 ÷ 7.

17 Find the value of:

    a $800 \div 200$ **b** $5400 \div 600$ **c** $7200 \div 900$

    d $18\,000 \div 3000$ **e** $45\,000 \div 5000$ **f** $102\,000 \div 2000$

18 Estimate the value of $1728 \div 38$.

1728 is closer to 1600 than 2000.

$$1728 \div 38 \approx 1600 \div 40$$
$$= 1600 \div 10 \div 4$$
$$= 160 \div 4$$
$$= 40$$

To estimate $1728 \div 38$, we round 38 to 40 and choose a number close to 1728 that can be divided by 40 exactly.

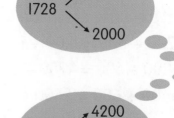

19 Estimate the value of $4367 \div 670$.

$$4367 \div 670 \approx \boxed{} \div 700$$
$$= \boxed{} \div \boxed{} \div 7$$
$$= \boxed{}$$

20 Estimate the value of the following:

    a $987 \div 17$ **b** $6106 \div 28$

    c $4932 \div 96$ **d** $3785 \div 379$

Activity

21 Find three whole numbers that can divide each of the numbers shown below exactly. The whole numbers must be multiples of tens, hundreds or thousands.

4500   **420**   **2000**   **40**   **88 000**

Draw and complete a table as shown below for each number.

Example

Number	Can be Divided By	Answer
4500	10	$4500 \div 10 = 450$
4500	30	$4500 \div 30 = 150$
4500	500	$4500 \div 500 = 9$

Let's Explore!

22 Work in pairs.

Discuss how you can work these out **without** using a calculator.

a   43 ÷ 10   b   735 ÷ 100   c   2046 ÷ 1000

Use the following chart to help you.

Thousands	Hundreds	Tens	Ones	•	Tenths	Hundredths	Thousandths

Let's Practise!

23 Find the value of:

a   870 ÷ 10   b   9000 ÷ 10   c   7100 ÷ 100

d   82 000 ÷ 100   e   3000 ÷ 1000   f   97 000 ÷ 1000

24 Find the value of:

a   500 ÷ 20   b   7070 ÷ 70   c   8100 ÷ 300

d   65 600 ÷ 800   e   6000 ÷ 3000   f   54 000 ÷ 9000

25   Use your calculator to work out the following:

a   6726 ÷ 19

b   4008 ÷ 12

Use estimation to check if your answers are reasonable.

Practice Book 5A, p.31

Let's Learn!

Order of operations

1 **Work from left to right when there's only addition and subtraction.**

In a primary school, there were 96 children in Year 1. The following year, 26 children left and 48 new children started. How many children were there in Year 2?

Working from left to right:

| First number sentence | $96 - 26 + 48$ |

96 – 26 + 48 is a number sentence.

| Second number sentence | $= 70 + 48$ |

$$= 118$$

There were 118 children in Year 2.

You can use your calculator to work out **96 – 26 + 48** like this:

Which operation was carried out first?
Which operation was carried out next?

Press	Display
C	0
9 6	96
– 2 6	26
+ 4 8	48
=	118

$96 - 26 + 48 = 118$

Home Maths Explain to your child that addition, subtraction, multiplication and division are called the four operations.

2 Work out the following. Then use your calculator to check your answers.

a 37 + 8 – 25   **b** 67 – 21 + 20

c 32 – 12 + 26 – 15   **d** 50 + 27 – 19 – 35

3 **Work from left to right when there's only multiplication and division.**

A shop owner ordered 40 boxes of fruit juice. Each box contained 24 cartons. He sells 60 cartons every day. How many days will he take to sell all the fruit juice?

Working from left to right:

First number sentence	40 × 24 ÷ 60
Second number sentence	= 960 ÷ 60
	= 16

He will take 16 days to sell all the fruit juice.

You can use your calculator to work out **40 × 24 ÷ 60** like this:

Which operation was carried out first?
Which operation was carried out next?

40 × 24 ÷ 60 = ◯

Press	Display
C	0
4 0	40
× 2 4	24
÷ 6 0	60
=	16

4 Work out the following. Then use your calculator to check your answers.

a 12 × 20 ÷ 6   **b** 63 ÷ 9 × 12

c 28 × 5 ÷ 10 ÷ 7   **d** 48 ÷ 8 × 60 ÷ 3

5 | **Carry out multiplication and division first, then work from left to right.**

There were 26 more children than women at a park. There were 4 times as many men as there were women. There were 56 men at the park. How many children were there?

Dividing first:

First number sentence	$26 + 56 \div 4$

Second number sentence	$= \quad 26 + 14$

$$= \quad 40$$

There were 40 children.

You can use your calculator to work out **26 + 56 ÷ 4** like this:

Which operation was carried out first?
Which operation was carried out next?

Press	Display
C	0
2 6	26
+ 5 6	56
÷ 4	4
=	40

$26 + 56 \div 4 = \boxed{}$

The calculator worked out **56 ÷ 4** first.
Then it worked out **26 + 14**.
It considers the order of operations automatically during computation.

Home Maths

Most everyday calculators, such as the ones on mobile phones, do not consider the order of operations automatically during calculations. A scientific calculator considers the order of operations automatically. Ask your child to type in 2 + 4 × 2 using the two types of calculators. They will get different answers: 12 and 10. The answer on a scientific calculator is correct because it follows the order of operations by calculating 4 × 2 before adding 2 to the result, while the other calculator adds 2 and 4 before multiplying the result by 2.

6 Peter had 900 stickers. He arranged 25 stickers on each page of an album. The album had 30 pages. How many stickers were left?

Multiplying first:

First number sentence	$900 - \mathbf{25 \times 30}$

Second number sentence	$= 900 - \mathbf{750}$

$$= \quad 150$$

There were 150 stickers left.

You can use your calculator to work out **900 − 25 × 30** like this:

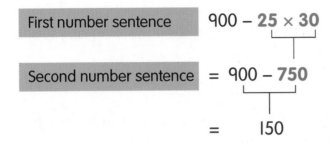

Press	Display
C	0
9 0 0	900
− 2 5	25
× 3 0	30
=	150

$900 - 25 \times 30 = \boxed{}$

Which operation did the calculator work out first? ⬜

Which operation did the calculator work out next? ⬜

7 Work out the following. Then use your calculator to check your answers.

a $13 + 20 \times 7$

b $70 - 75 \div 5$

c $15 + 18 \times 5 \div 9$

d $80 - 54 \div 9 \times 11$

e $48 - 6 \times 6 + 34$

f $33 + 210 \div 30 - 25$

Let's Explore!

8 Work in pairs.

Each pair will need a scientific calculator and a standard calculator.

1 Using the scientific calculator, work out the following questions. Start with the operation on the left.

   a   178 − 25 × 6   **b**   85 + 120 ÷ 8

2 Next use the standard calculator to work out **a** and **b**. Are the answers you get on both calculators the same?

3 Write the order of operations carried out in **a** and **b** using

   i   the scientific calculator   **ii**   the standard calculator.

Which calculator gave the correct answers?

9 **When there are brackets, carry out the operations in the brackets first.**

There are 670 red seats and 530 blue seats in a theatre. Each row has 40 seats. How many rows are there in the theatre?

Work out the operation in the brackets first:

First number sentence	(670 + 530) ÷ 40

Second number sentence	= 1200 ÷ 40

=   30

There are 30 rows in the theatre.

You can use your calculator to work out **(670 + 530) ÷ 40** like this:

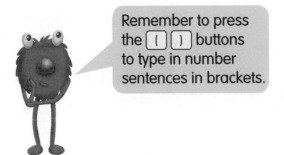

Remember to press the ( ) buttons to type in number sentences in brackets.

Press	Display
C	0
(6 7 0	[6 7 0
+ 5 3 0)	5 3 0]
÷ 4 0	4 0
=	3 0

(670 + 530) ÷ 40 = ⬡

Which operation did the calculator work out first? ⬡
Which operation did the calculator work out next? ⬡

10 Work out the following. Then use your calculator to check your answers.

a 17 − (38 − 29)   b 690 ÷ (15 × 2)
c 107 + (44 − 33) × 7   d 80 × (40 ÷ 5) ÷ 10

Activity

11 Work in pairs.

Prepare three sets of number cards (0 to 9), operation cards (+, −, ×, ÷) and bracket cards.

0 1 2 3 4 5 6 7 8 9 + − × ÷ ( )

Use the cards to make a number sentence with two or more operations.

Example

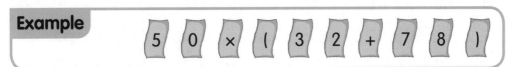

5 0 × (3 2 + 7 8)

Use your calculator to work out the answer and compare your answer with your partner's answer.

Let's Explore!

12 To find the value of 1350 × 27 ÷ 25, use your calculator to work out 1350 × 27 first. Then divide the result by 25.

Next use your calculator to work out 27 ÷ 25 first. Then multiply the result by 1350. What do you notice? Try with other numbers.

13 Work in groups of three.

Look at the five number sentences in the table below.
Pupil A is to work them out from left to right **without** using a calculator.
Pupil B is to work them out according to the rules of order of operations **without** using a calculator.
Pupil C is to work them out using a calculator by typing in the number sentences from left to right.

Copy the table and record your answers as shown. Discuss your results.

Number Sentence	Pupil A's Answers	Pupil B's Answers	Pupil C's Answers
9 + 6 − 5			
48 ÷ 4 × 2			
36 ÷ 6 − 3			
14 + 4 × 2			
50 − 8 ÷ 2			

Let's Practise!

14 Find the value of the following. Then use your calculator to check your answers.

a   96 − 50 + 64

b   175 + 25 − 95

c   6 × 40 ÷ 3

d   250 ÷ 5 × 53

e   79 + 27 × 2

f   280 − 72 ÷ 8

g   35 × (560 ÷ 70)

h   540 ÷ (293 − 203)

Practice Book 5A, p.35

Let's Learn!

Word problems (I)

1 🖩 An artist wants to make a picture using tiles mounted on a rectangular board measuring 103 cm by 59 cm.

  a What is the area of the board?
  b Each tile costs £12. How much will it cost to cover the board completely with 1 cm² tiles?

  a Area = Length × Width
  = 103 × 59
  = 6077 cm²

Estimate the answer
103 × 59 ≈ 100 × 60
= 6000
6077 is a reasonable answer.

The area of the board is 6077 cm².

  b Cost of tiling = area × cost of 1 cm² tile
  = 6077 × £12
  = £72 924

Estimate to check if the answer is reasonable.

It will cost £72 924 to cover the board completely with the tiles.

2 A container can hold 450 cm³ of orange juice. Mr Thomas has to fill 19 of these containers with orange juice at 15 p per cm³. How much does he have to pay altogether?

Total amount of orange juice = 450 cm³ × 19 = ⬚

Cost of orange juice = ⬚ × 15 p = £⬚

He would have to pay £⬚.

3 Mr James bought 32 boxes of stickers. There were 140 stickers in each box. He packed them into bags of 35 stickers each. He sold each bag for 98 p. How much money did he make after selling all the stickers?

First find the total number of stickers.

Total number of stickers = number of boxes × number of stickers in each box
= 32 × 140
= 4480

There were 4480 stickers.

Next find the number of bags.

Number of bags = total number of stickers ÷ number of stickers in each bag
= 4480 ÷ 35
= 128

There are 128 bags of stickers.

(32 × 140) ÷ 35
= ⬚

Then find how much money he collected.

Amount collected = number of bags × cost of each bag
= 128 × 98 p
= ⬚ p
= £⬚

He collected £⬚.

4 Miya's uncle buys a boat and pays for it in instalments.
Each instalment is £1235. After paying 64 instalments, he still
has to pay another £2960. How much would each instalment be
if he pays for the boat in 100 instalments?

First find the total amount paid in instalments.

Amount paid = number of instalments × amount for each instalment

= 64 × £1235

= £⬚

Then find the cost of the boat.

Cost of boat = total amount paid + amount he still has to pay

= £⬚ + £2960

= £⬚

(64 × £1235) + £2960

= £⬚

What operation do you need to carry out to find out how much he would
have to pay for each of the 100 instalments?

£⬚ ◯ ⬚ = £⬚

He would have to pay £⬚ for each of the 100 instalments.

5 The table on the right shows how much it costs to hire a stall in a market.

Weekdays	£32 per day
Saturdays and Sundays	£55 per day

Peter's dad had a stall from Tuesday to the following Monday. How much did it cost him?

First find the number of weekdays and the number of Saturdays and Sundays he hired the stall.

Number of weekdays he hired the stall = 5 days

Number of Saturdays and Sundays he hired the stall = 2 days

Cost of the stall for 5 weekdays = 5 × £32 = £160

Cost of the stall for Saturday and Sunday = 2 × £55 = £110

Total cost = £160 + £110 = £270

(5 × £32) + (2 × £55)

= £270

Hiring the stall cost him £270.

6 The table shows the charges at a car park.

First Hour	Second Hour	After the Second Hour
free	£1	£2 per hour

Mrs Lee parked her car at the car park from 9:00 a.m. to 2:00 p.m. on the same day. How much did she have to pay?

Total number of hours = ⬜h

Parking fee for first hour = £⬜

Parking fee for second hour = £⬜

Parking fee from 11:00 a.m. to 2:00 p.m. = ⬜ × £⬜ = £⬜

Total parking fee = £⬜ + £⬜ + £⬜ = £⬜

Mrs Lee had to pay £⬜.

Let's Practise!

Solve these word problems. Show your workings clearly.

7 Ruby's mum sold 78 boxes of raffle tickets. Each box contained 34 books of tickets. She sold each book for £17. How much did she collect altogether?

8 A supermarket had a total of 6707 tins of food. They sold 569 of the tins. Then they put the remaining tins equally into 18 crates. How many tins were there in each crate?

9 A greengrocer had 49 boxes of strawberries. Each box contained 75 strawberries. The strawberries were repacked into packets of 15. How many packets of strawberries were there?

10 Mr Marsh paid £2 for a packet of 12 buns. He sold each bun for 50 pence. In a week, he sold a total of 4385 buns.
   a What was the smallest number of packets of buns he bought?
   b How much did he pay for this number of packets of buns?
   c How much money did he make after he sold 4385 buns?

11 A restaurant owner bought 245 boxes of tinned tomatoes. Each box contained 28 tins of tomatoes. There were 2198 tins of whole tomatoes and the rest were chopped tomatoes. All the tins of chopped tomatoes were used over 42 months. If the restaurant owner used the same number of tins of chopped tomatoes each month, how many tins of chopped tomatoes did he use each month?

12 The table on the right shows the cost of sending parcels.

Tai and Miya sent parcels.

Mass	Postage
First 20 g	70 p
Per additional 10 g	30 p

   a Tai posted a parcel with a mass of 45 g. Find the postage for the parcel.
   b Miya paid £6·10 for posting a parcel. Find the mass of the parcel.

> Practice Book 5A, p.41

Let's Learn!

Word problems (2)

1 Omar, Farha and Jack scored a total of 4670 points during a competition. Farha scored 316 fewer points than Omar. Farha scored 3 times as many points as Jack. How many points did Farha score?

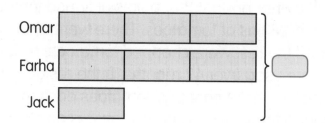

First subtract 316 points from Omar's score so that he will have the same number of points as Farha. This is the same as subtracting 316 points from the total number of points.

4670 − 316 = ☐

Then Omar has 3 units, Farha has 3 units and Jack has 1 unit. In all, they have 7 units.

7 units ⟶ ☐ points

1 unit ⟶ ☐ ÷ 7 = ☐ points

3 units ⟶ 3 × ☐ = ☐ points

Farha scored ☐ points.

2 🖩 The cost of 4 belts and 5 ties was £247. Each tie cost 3 times as much as a belt. What was the total cost of a tie and a belt?

Draw models. Represent 1 belt with 1 unit and 1 tie with 3 units.

4 belts

5 ties

£ ☐

☐ units ⟶ £247

1 unit ⟶ £247 ÷ ☐ = £ ☐

Each belt cost £ ☐.

3 units ⟶ 3 × £ ☐ = £39

Each tie cost £ ☐.

£ ☐ + £ ☐ = £ ☐

The total cost of a belt and a tie was £ ☐.

3 Mr Austin had an equal number of red and yellow tulips. He sold 624 red tulips. Then there were 4 times as many yellow tulips as red tulips. How many tulips did he have at first?

Before

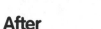
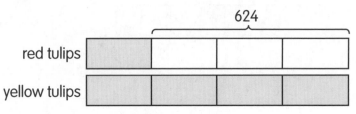

red tulips

yellow tulips

?

After

624

red tulips

yellow tulips

I unit represents the number of red tulips left and 4 units represent the number of yellow tulips.

3 units ⟶ 624 tulips
I unit ⟶ 624 ÷ 3 = 208 tulips
8 units ⟶ 8 × ⬚ = ⬚ tulips

He had ⬚ tulips at first.

4 A greengrocer bought 588 mangoes at 4 for £5. She then sold all of them at 7 for £10. How much money did she make?

588 ÷ 4 = 147
147 × £5 = £735

She bought the mangoes for £735.

How many groups of 4 are there in 588?

How many groups of 7 are there in 588?

588 ÷ 7 = 84
84 × £10 = £840

She sold them for £840.

£840 − £735 = £105

She made £105.

5 Miss Bell and Mr Michaels had £1250. Miss Bell and Mrs Campbell had £830. Mr Michaels had 4 times as much as Mrs Campbell. How much did Miss Bell have?

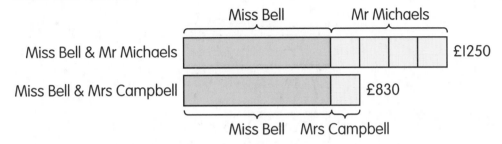

£1250 – £830 = £420

The difference between the amount Mr Michaels and Mrs Campbell had was £420.

3 units ⟶ £420
1 unit ⟶ £420 ÷ 3 = £⬭

Mrs Campbell had £⬭.

£830 – £⬭ = £⬭

Miss Bell had £⬭.

6 Mary is 12 years old and Abby is 15 years older than her. In how many years' time will Abby be twice as old as Mary?

Method 1

12 + 15 = 27

Abby is 27 years old now.

Mary's Age	Abby's Age	Is it Twice?
12 (now)	27 (now)	No
13	28	No
14	29	No
15	30	Yes

We can guess and check for this question. Start by making a systematic list.

Abby will be twice Mary's age in 3 years' time.

Method 2

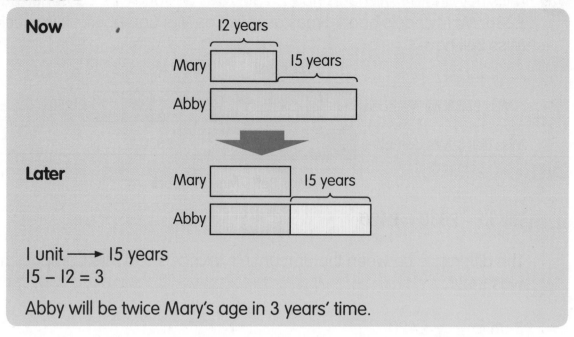

Now

Mary 12 years

Abby 15 years

Later

Mary 15 years

Abby

I unit ⟶ 15 years

15 − 12 = 3

Abby will be twice Mary's age in 3 years' time.

7 There are 20 cars and motorbikes altogether in a car park. The total number of wheels is 50. How many motorbikes are there?

Use the data — number of vehicles and number of wheels — to make guesses and a systematic list.

Remember, the number of cars and motorbikes must always add up to 20.

Number of Cars	Number of Motorbikes	Number of Wheels	Are there 50 Wheels?
10	10	40 + 20 = 60	No (too many)
9	11	⬚	No (too many)
⬚	12	32 + 24 = 56	No (too many)
5	15	20 + 30 = 50	⬚

There are ⬚ motorbikes.

Let's Practise!

Solve these word problems. Show your workings clearly.

8 Mr Williams gave a total sum of £3600 to his brother and 2 sisters. His brother received £500 more than the first sister. The second sister received half as much as the first sister. How much did the first sister receive?

9 Apples are sold at 3 for £2 at Stall A. At Stall B, the same apples are sold at 5 for £2. Daniel buys 15 apples from Stall B instead of Stall A. How much does he save?

10 Mr Jacobs paid £87 altogether for a pair of boots and a pair of shoes. The boots cost twice as much as the shoes. What was the cost of the boots?

11 A shopkeeper sold 15 boxes of pencils altogether on Monday and Tuesday. He sold 3 more boxes on Monday than on Tuesday. There were 12 pencils in each box. How many pencils did he sell on Monday?

12 Ella had £7 and her sister had £2. After their parents gave each of them an equal amount of money, Ella had twice as much as her sister. How much did their parents give each of them?

13 A group of people paid £720 altogether for tickets to an amusement park. The price of a ticket for an adult was £15 and the price for a child was £8. There were 25 more adults than children. How many children were there in the group?

14 A tank and a bucket contained a total of 8346 ml of water. When 314 ml of water was poured from the bucket into the tank, the amount of water in the tank was 12 times that in the bucket. How much water was in the bucket at first?

Practice Book 5A, p.45

Let's Wrap It Up!

You have learnt to:

- use a calculator to add, subtract, multiply and divide
- multiply and divide a whole number by 10, 100 and 1000
- multiply and divide a whole number by tens, hundreds and thousands
- use rounding and approximation to estimate the products and quotients
- work out a number sentence using the correct order of operations.

Let's Revise!

Miss Austin bought 48 packets of red balloons, 66 packets of blue balloons and 35 packets of yellow balloons. Each packet cost £3 and contained a dozen balloons. She mixed them up and gave away 213 balloons. Then she repacked the remainder into packets of 25 balloons each.

a How many balloons did Miss Austin buy altogether?

$$(48 + 66 + 35) \times 12 = 149 \times 12$$
$$= 1788$$

She bought 1788 balloons altogether.

b How many packets of balloons did she repack?

$$(1788 - 213) \div 25 = 1575 \div 25$$
$$= 63$$

She repacked 63 packets of balloons.

c If she sold each repacked packet of 25 balloons at £10 each, how much money did she make?

$$63 \times £10 - 149 \times £3 = £630 - £447$$
$$= £183$$

She made £183.

Put On Your Thinking Caps!

15 The 9 button on a calculator is not working.

Explain how you can use this calculator to work out 1234 × 79 in at least two different ways.

Practice Book 5A, p.49

Practice Book 5A, p.51

Unit 3 Fractions (I)

Let's Learn!

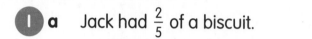

1 **a** Jack had $\frac{2}{5}$ of a biscuit. Ella had $\frac{3}{5}$ of a biscuit.

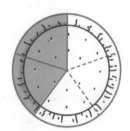 

$\frac{2}{5}$ and $\frac{3}{5}$ are **like fractions**.

They have the same denominator, 5.

b Peter had $\frac{2}{3}$ of a pizza. Ruby had $\frac{3}{4}$ of a pizza.

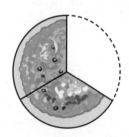 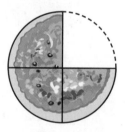

$\frac{2}{3}$ and $\frac{3}{4}$ are **unlike fractions**.

They have different denominators, 3 and 4.

Let's Learn!

Adding unlike fractions

1 $\frac{1}{2}$ of a stick is painted red. $\frac{1}{3}$ of the stick is painted green. What fraction of the stick is painted red and green?

$$\frac{1}{2} + \frac{1}{3} = ?$$

Add $\frac{1}{2}$ and $\frac{1}{3}$.

To add, convert $\frac{1}{2}$ and $\frac{1}{3}$ to like fractions.

List the multiples of the denominators, 2 and 3.

Multiples of 2: **2** , **4** , **6** , **8** , …

Multiples of 3: **3** , **6** , **9** , **12** , …

6 is the lowest common multiple of 2 and 3.

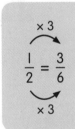

$\frac{1}{2}$ and $\frac{3}{6}$ are **equivalent fractions**.

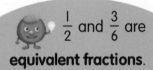

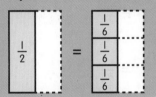

$\frac{1}{2} = \frac{3}{6}$ $\frac{1}{3} = \frac{2}{6}$

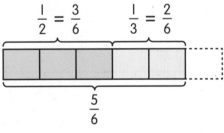

$$\frac{5}{6}$$

As 6 is the lowest common multiple, I draw a model with 6 units.

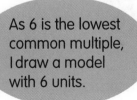

$$\frac{1}{2} + \frac{1}{3} = \frac{3}{6} + \frac{2}{6}$$
$$= \frac{5}{6}$$

$\frac{5}{6}$ of the stick is painted red and green.

2 Add $\frac{1}{2}$ and $\frac{2}{7}$.

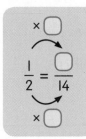

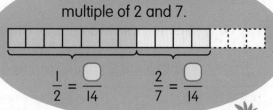

14 is the lowest common multiple of 2 and 7.

$\frac{1}{2} = \frac{\square}{14}$ $\frac{2}{7} = \frac{\square}{14}$

$\frac{1}{2} + \frac{2}{7} = \frac{\square}{14} + \frac{\square}{14}$

$= \frac{\square}{\square}$

3 Find the sum of $\frac{1}{4}$ and $\frac{1}{3}$.

What is a common multiple of 4 and 3?

$\frac{1}{4} = \frac{\square}{\square}$ $\frac{1}{3} = \frac{\square}{\square}$

$\frac{1}{4} + \frac{1}{3} = \frac{\square}{\square} + \frac{\square}{\square}$

$= \frac{\square}{\square}$

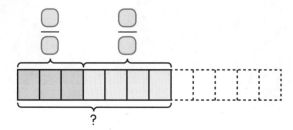

?

Activity

4 Draw bars to show the sum of these fractions. Then find the sum of the fractions.

a $\frac{1}{2} + \frac{1}{4}$ b $\frac{1}{5} + \frac{3}{4}$ c $\frac{1}{4} + \frac{2}{3}$

Maths Journal

5 One of the three models below shows the sum of $\frac{1}{2}$ and $\frac{1}{7}$. The other two models are incorrect. Explain why they are incorrect.

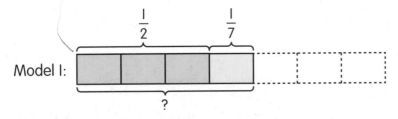

Model I:

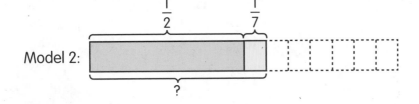

Model 2:

Model 3:

Let's Practise!

6 Draw a model to find the sum of each pair of fractions.

a $\frac{1}{2}$ and $\frac{2}{5}$ b $\frac{1}{3}$ and $\frac{1}{4}$ c $\frac{3}{5}$ and $\frac{1}{3}$

7 Add. Express the answer in its simplest form where necessary.

a $\frac{2}{3} + \frac{1}{8}$ b $\frac{2}{3} + \frac{1}{12}$ c $\frac{1}{5} + \frac{3}{10}$ d $\frac{1}{4} + \frac{1}{6}$

Practice Book 5A, p.65

Let's Learn!

Subtracting unlike fractions

1 Bottle A contained $\frac{3}{4}\ell$ of milk. Tai poured $\frac{1}{6}\ell$ of it into Bottle B.
How much milk was left in Bottle A?

$$\frac{3}{4} - \frac{1}{6} = ?$$

List the multiples of the denominators, 4 and 6.

Subtract $\frac{1}{6}\ell$ from $\frac{3}{4}\ell$ of milk.

To subtract, convert $\frac{1}{6}$ and $\frac{3}{4}$ to like fractions first.

Multiples of 4:   **4** , **8** , **12** , **16**, …

Multiples of 6:   **6** , **12** , **18** , **24**, …

12 is the lowest common multiple of 4 and 6.

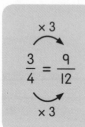

$$\begin{array}{c} \times 3 \\ \frac{3}{4} = \frac{9}{12} \\ \times 3 \end{array} \qquad \begin{array}{c} \times 2 \\ \frac{1}{6} = \frac{2}{12} \\ \times 2 \end{array}$$

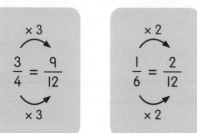

$$\frac{3}{4} = \frac{9}{12}$$

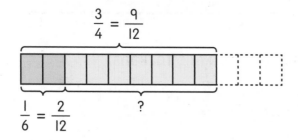

$$\frac{1}{6} = \frac{2}{12} \qquad ?$$

As 12 is the lowest common multiple, I draw a model with 12 units.

$$\frac{3}{4} - \frac{1}{6} = \frac{9}{12} - \frac{2}{12}$$

$$= \frac{7}{12}\ell$$

$\frac{7}{12}\ell$ of milk was left in Bottle A.

2 Subtract $\frac{1}{5}$ from $\frac{2}{3}$.

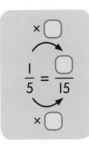 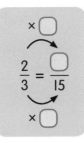

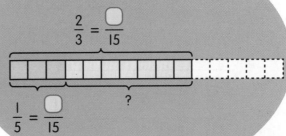

15 is the lowest common multiple of 3 and 5.

$\frac{2}{3} = \frac{\square}{15}$

$\frac{1}{5} = \frac{\square}{15}$

$\frac{2}{3} - \frac{1}{5} = \frac{\square}{15} - \frac{\square}{15}$

$\qquad = \frac{\square}{15}$

3 Find the difference between $\frac{5}{6}$ and $\frac{5}{9}$.

$\frac{5}{6} = \frac{\square}{\square}$ $\qquad$ $\frac{5}{9} = \frac{\square}{\square}$

What is the lowest common multiple of 6 and 9?

$\frac{5}{6} - \frac{5}{9} = \frac{\square}{\square} - \frac{\square}{\square}$

$\qquad = \frac{\square}{\square}$

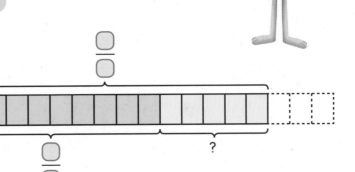

Activity

4 Draw bars to show the difference between the fractions. Then find the difference between the fractions.

a $\frac{1}{2} - \frac{2}{7}$ $\qquad$ b $\frac{5}{6} - \frac{4}{9}$ $\qquad$ c $\frac{3}{4} - \frac{3}{5}$

Let's Practise!

5. Complete the model with the fractions $\frac{1}{2}$, $\frac{3}{10}$ and $\frac{4}{5}$. Then write two subtraction sentences.

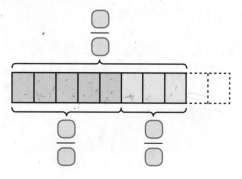

6. Subtract. Draw models to help you.

   a $\frac{5}{8} - \frac{1}{2}$ **b** $\frac{4}{5} - \frac{1}{4}$

7. Subtract. Express your answer in its simplest form.

   a $\frac{5}{6} - \frac{1}{12}$ **b** $\frac{9}{10} - \frac{3}{5}$

   c $\frac{8}{9} - \frac{5}{6}$ **d** $\frac{11}{12} - \frac{7}{8}$

   e $\frac{4}{5} - \frac{2}{7}$ **f** $\frac{7}{9} - \frac{3}{4}$

   g $\frac{4}{7} - \frac{1}{6}$ **h** $\frac{2}{3} - \frac{3}{8}$

Practice Book 5A, p.69

Let's Learn!

Fractions and division

1 2 identical pizzas are shared equally among 3 pupils.
What fraction of a pizza will.each pupil get?

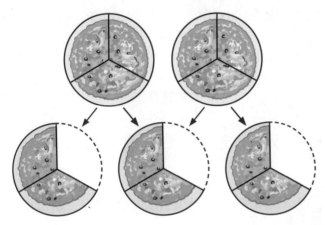

Each pizza is divided into 3 parts equally.
Each part is $\frac{1}{3}$ of a pizza.

$2 \div 3 = \frac{2}{3}$

2 divided by 3 is the same as $\frac{2}{3}$.

Each pupil will get $\frac{2}{3}$ of a pizza.

2 3 identical muffins were cut and shared among 4 children after dinner.
What fraction of a muffin did each child get?

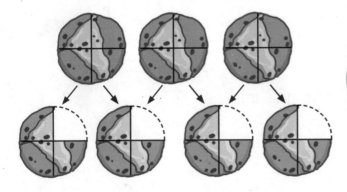

Each muffin is divided into ☐ equal parts.

Each part is $\frac{\square}{\square}$ of a muffin.

$3 \div 4 = \frac{\square}{\square}$

Each child got $\frac{\square}{\square}$ of a muffin.

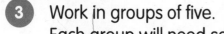

Activity

3   Work in groups of five.
Each group will need some paper strips of the same size and length.
The number of paper strips must be fewer than the number of pupils
in your group.

    I   Cut the strips into equal pieces so that each pupil gets the same
          number of pieces.

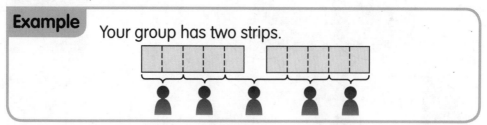

Example   Your group has two strips.

    2   Write the fraction of a strip that each one of you gets. For the
          example in **I**, write: $2 \div 5 = \dfrac{2}{5}$

---

4   Find the value of each of the following. Express your answer as a fraction.

    a $4 \div 5 = \dfrac{\square}{\square}$ **b** $7 \div 9 = \dfrac{\square}{\square}$

    c $5 \div 8 = \dfrac{\square}{\square}$ **d** $7 \div 11 = \dfrac{\square}{\square}$

5   Express each fraction as a division sentence.

    a $\dfrac{3}{7} = \square \div \square$ **b** $\dfrac{8}{12} = \square \div \square$

    c $\dfrac{3}{10} = \square \div \square$ **d** $\dfrac{5}{6} = \square \div \square$

6 5 identical pancakes are divided equally among 4 pupils. How many pancakes does each pupil get?

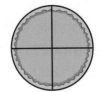 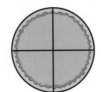 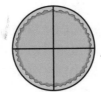 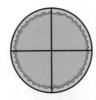

Each pancake is divided into 4 parts equally.

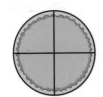   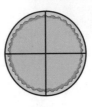

Method I

$$5 \div 4 = \frac{5}{4}$$
$$= \frac{4}{4} + \frac{1}{4}$$
$$= 1\frac{1}{4}$$

 Recall that:

$$\frac{5}{4} = 5 \text{ fourths}$$
$$= 4 \text{ fourths} + 1 \text{ fourth}$$
$$= \frac{4}{4} + \frac{1}{4}$$
$$= 1\frac{1}{4}$$

We usually call fourths, **quarters**.

Method 2

$$\begin{array}{r} 1 \\ 4\overline{)5} \\ -4 \\ \hline 1 \end{array}$$ $$5 \div 4 = 1\frac{1}{4}$$

5 divided by 4 is the same as $\frac{5}{4}$ or $1\frac{1}{4}$.

Each pupil gets $1\frac{1}{4}$ pancakes.

Activity

7 Work in groups.
Each group will need some paper strips of the same size and length. The number of paper strips must be one more than the number of pupils in your group. For example, if your group has three pupils, the group should get four paper strips.

I Cut the strips into equal pieces so that each of you gets the same number of pieces.

Example

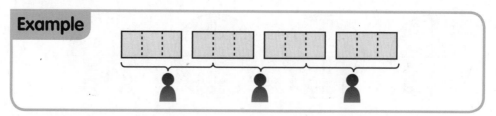

2 First write a division sentence and express it as a fraction to show what each of you gets. Then write the fraction as a mixed number.
For the example in **I**, write: $4 \div 3 = \dfrac{4}{3}$
$$= 1\dfrac{1}{3}$$

8 Express $14 \div 4$ as a fraction in its simplest form. Then change the fraction to a mixed number.

$14 \div 4 = \dfrac{\overset{7}{\cancel{14}}}{\underset{2}{\cancel{4}}}$

$= \dfrac{7}{2}$

$= 3\dfrac{1}{2}$

$$\begin{array}{r} 3 \\ 2{\overline{\smash{\big)}\,7}} \\ \underline{-6} \\ 1 \end{array}$$

9 Express each division sentence as a fraction in its simplest form. Then change the fraction to a mixed number.

a $19 \div 2$ b $43 \div 4$ c $49 \div 5$ d $20 \div 8$

10 Follow the steps to type in fractions and mixed numbers on your calculator.

Turn your calculator on.

To type in $\frac{1}{2}$, press: $\boxed{1}$ $\boxed{a^{b/c}}$ $\boxed{2}$

To clear the display on your calculator, press: $\boxed{C}$

To type in $2\frac{3}{5}$, press: $\boxed{2}$ $\boxed{a^{b/c}}$ $\boxed{3}$ $\boxed{a^{b/c}}$ $\boxed{5}$

Display

| 0 |
| $\frac{1}{2}$ |
| 0 |
| $2\frac{3}{5}$ |

Let's Practise!

11 Find the value of each of the following. Express your answer as a fraction in its simplest form or as a mixed number.

a $10 \div 12 = \dfrac{\square}{\square}$

$= \dfrac{\square}{\square}$

b $3 \div 2 = \dfrac{3}{2}$

$= \dfrac{\square}{\square} + \dfrac{\square}{\square}$

$= \square\dfrac{\square}{\square}$

c $7 \div 3$ d $\dfrac{11}{4}$ e $\dfrac{25}{7}$

Practice Book 5A, p.73

Let's Learn!

Converting fractions to decimals

Converting tenths, hundredths and thousandths

1 Express $\frac{2}{5}$ as a decimal.

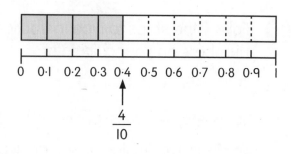

$$\frac{2}{5} = \frac{2 \times 2}{5 \times 2}$$

$$= \frac{4}{10}$$

$$= 0 \cdot 4$$

$\frac{4}{10}$

2 Express $\frac{9}{20}$ as a decimal.

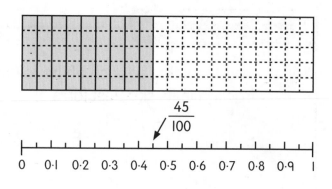

$$\frac{9}{20} = \frac{9 \times 5}{20 \times 5}$$

$$= \frac{45}{100}$$

$$= 0 \cdot 45$$

$\frac{45}{100}$

3 Express $\frac{1}{8}$ as a decimal.

$$\frac{1}{8} = \frac{1 \times 125}{8 \times 125}$$

$$= \frac{125}{1000}$$

$$= 0 \cdot 125$$

8 is a factor of 1000.
$8 \times 125 = 1000$

By converting $\frac{1}{8}$ to $\frac{125}{1000}$, we can express the fraction as a decimal easily.

4 Convert each fraction to a decimal.

a $\frac{4}{5} = \frac{8}{10} = \boxed{}$

b $\frac{7}{20} = \frac{35}{100} = \boxed{}$

c $\frac{2}{8} = \boxed{}$

d $\frac{6}{8} = \boxed{}$

Converting using long division

5 Express $\frac{3}{7}$ as a decimal. Round your answer to 2 decimal places.

$\frac{3}{7} = 3 \div 7$

≈ 0.43

$$
\begin{array}{r}
0.428 \\
7\overline{)\,3} \\
-28 \\
\hline
20 \\
-14 \\
\hline
60 \\
-56 \\
\hline
4
\end{array}
$$

Why do we need to find the answer to 3 decimal places first?

6 Express $\frac{2}{9}$ as a decimal. Round your answer to 2 decimal places.

$\frac{2}{9} = 2 \div 9$

$\approx \boxed{}$

$$
\begin{array}{r}
0.22\boxed{} \\
9\overline{)\,2} \\
-18 \\
\hline
20 \\
-18 \\
\hline
2\boxed{} \\
-\boxed{}\boxed{} \\
\hline
\boxed{}
\end{array}
$$

7 Convert each fraction to a decimal. Round your answers to 2 decimal places.

a $\frac{5}{7} \approx \boxed{}$

b $\frac{1}{6} \approx \boxed{}$

c $\frac{2}{3} \approx \boxed{}$

d $\frac{8}{9} \approx \boxed{}$

Activity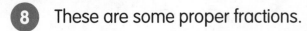

8 These are some proper fractions.

$$\frac{1}{2}, \frac{2}{3}, \frac{3}{4}, \frac{3}{5}, \frac{5}{6}, \frac{2}{7}, \frac{7}{8}, \frac{2}{9}, \frac{3}{10}, \frac{6}{11}, \frac{11}{12}$$

Use your calculator to find the fractions that have:

a 1, 2 or 3 decimal places when expressed as decimals.

b more than 3 decimal places when expressed as decimals.

9 Write the following as decimals. Round your answers to 2 decimal places if necessary.

a $\frac{3}{11}$ **b** $\frac{7}{15}$ **c** $\frac{2}{13}$ **d** $\frac{11}{21}$

Converting improper fractions and mixed numbers

10 Express $9 \div 6$ as a decimal.

$$9 \div 6 = \frac{9}{6}$$
$$= 1 + \frac{3}{6}$$
$$= 1 \cdot 5$$

$$\begin{array}{r} 0 \cdot 5 \\ 6\overline{)\,3} \\ -3\,0 \\ \hline 0 \end{array}$$

11 Express $2\frac{1}{7}$ as a decimal. Round your answer to 2 decimal places.

$$2\frac{1}{7} = 2 + \frac{1}{7}$$
$$\approx 2 + 0 \cdot 14$$
$$= 2 \cdot 14$$

$$\begin{array}{r} 0 \cdot 142 \\ 7\overline{)\,1} \\ -\ 7 \\ \hline 30 \\ -28 \\ \hline 20 \\ -14 \\ \hline 6 \end{array}$$

12 Write the following as decimals. Round your answers to 2 decimal places if necessary.

   a $12 \div 5$ **b** $8 \div 3$ **c** $3\frac{3}{5}$ **d** $5\frac{7}{9}$

13 Express the following as decimals. Round your answers to 2 decimal places if necessary.

   a $\frac{13}{9} \approx 1\cdot44$

      Turn your calculator on.

      To convert $\frac{13}{9}$, press $\boxed{1}$ $\boxed{3}$ $\boxed{\div}$ $\boxed{9}$ $\boxed{=}$

Display

0

1·4444 . . .

   b $5\frac{4}{7} = 5 + \frac{4}{7} \approx \boxed{}$

      To clear the display on your calculator, press $\boxed{C}$

      To convert $\frac{4}{7}$, press $\boxed{4}$ $\boxed{\div}$ $\boxed{7}$ $\boxed{=}$

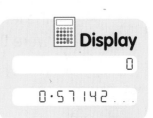

Display

0

0·57142 . . .

14 Express the following as decimals. Round your answers to 2 decimal places if necessary.

   a $\frac{19}{6}$ **b** $7\frac{9}{17}$ **c** $4\frac{5}{18}$ **d** $10\frac{8}{23}$

Let's Practise!

15 Express each fraction as a decimal.

   a $\frac{3}{5}$ **b** $\frac{17}{20}$ **c** $\frac{5}{8}$

Let's Practise!

16 Convert the following fractions to decimals. Round your answers to 2 decimal places.

a $\dfrac{1}{9}$ **b** $\dfrac{2}{7}$ **c** $\dfrac{7}{11}$

17 Read each question. Write a division sentence. Then solve the problem.

a 8 identical cakes were shared equally among 6 children. How many cakes did each child get?

b Jeff made 16 ℓ of lemonade in a big container. He then poured the lemonade equally into 5 jugs. How many litres of lemonade were there in each jug? Express your answer as:

    i a mixed number   **ii** a decimal.

18 Find the value of each of the following. Express your answer as a mixed number and as a decimal correct to 2 decimal places.

a $7 \div 6$ **b** $13 \div 9$ **c** $\dfrac{14}{5}$ **d** $\dfrac{45}{11}$

19 Express each fraction or mixed number as a decimal. Round your answer to 2 decimal places where necessary.

a $\dfrac{7}{13}$ **b** $\dfrac{21}{35}$ **c** $\dfrac{22}{80}$

d $3\dfrac{5}{18}$ **e** $2\dfrac{7}{12}$ **f** $5\dfrac{4}{15}$

Practice Book 5A, p.77

Let's Learn!

Adding mixed numbers

1 Susie walked $1\frac{1}{2}$ km and jogged $2\frac{3}{4}$ km. How many kilometres did she walk and jog altogether?

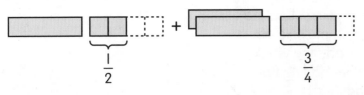

$$3\frac{5}{4} = 3 + \frac{4}{4} + \frac{1}{4}$$

$$= 3 + 1 + \frac{1}{4}$$

$$= 4\frac{1}{4}$$

$\times 2$

$$\frac{1}{2} = \frac{2}{4}$$

$\times 2$

I can also simplify $3\frac{5}{4}$ this way:

$$\begin{array}{r} 1 \\ 4\overline{)5} \\ -4 \\ \hline 1 \end{array}$$

$$\frac{5}{4} = 1\frac{1}{4}$$

$$3\frac{5}{4} = 3 + 1\frac{1}{4}$$

$$= 4\frac{1}{4}$$

$$1\frac{1}{2} + 2\frac{3}{4} = 1\frac{2}{4} + 2\frac{3}{4}$$

$$= 3\frac{5}{4}$$

$$= 4\frac{1}{4} \text{ km}$$

Susie walked and jogged $4\frac{1}{4}$ km altogether.

2 Find the sum of $2\frac{2}{3}$ and $3\frac{5}{9}$.

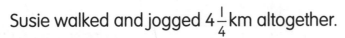

$\times 3$

$$\frac{2}{3} = \frac{\Box}{9}$$

$\times 3$

$$2\frac{2}{3} + 3\frac{5}{9} = 2\frac{\Box}{\Box} + 3\frac{\Box}{\Box}$$

$$= 5\frac{\Box}{9}$$

$$= \Box\frac{\Box}{\Box}$$

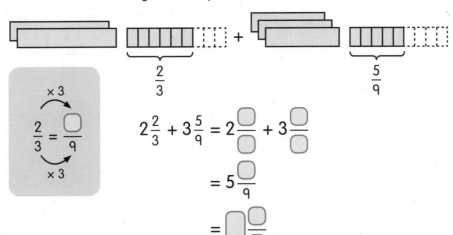

3 Ruby bought $2\frac{1}{5}$ kg of pears. She also bought $1\frac{1}{2}$ kg of grapes.
What is the total mass of fruit that she bought?

$$2\frac{1}{5} + 1\frac{1}{2} = ?$$

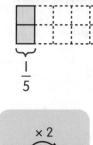

First convert the fractional parts to like fractions. 10 is the lowest common multiple of 5 and 2. Then add the whole numbers before adding the fractional parts.

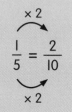

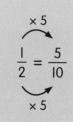

$$2\frac{1}{5} + 1\frac{1}{2} = 2\frac{2}{10} + 1\frac{5}{10}$$

$$= 3\frac{7}{10} \text{ kg}$$

Ruby bought $3\frac{7}{10}$ kg of fruit.

4 Add $3\frac{1}{4}$ and $2\frac{5}{9}$.

$$3\frac{1}{4} + 2\frac{5}{9} = 3\frac{\bigcirc}{\bigcirc} + 2\frac{\bigcirc}{\bigcirc}$$

$$= \bigcirc\frac{\bigcirc}{\bigcirc}$$

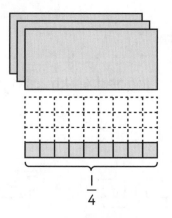

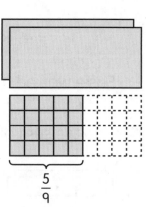

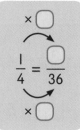

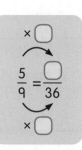

Activity

5 Work in pairs.

a Write two mixed numbers with denominator 3 that have a sum of $5\frac{2}{3}$.

$$\bigcirc\frac{\bigcirc}{3} + \bigcirc\frac{\bigcirc}{3} = 5\frac{2}{3}$$

b Write two mixed numbers with denominator 4 that have a sum of $3\frac{3}{4}$.

$$\bigcirc\frac{\bigcirc}{4} + \bigcirc\frac{\bigcirc}{4} = 3\frac{3}{4}$$

6 Find the sum of $3\frac{2}{5}$ and $4\frac{7}{8}$. Express your answer as:

a a mixed number   **b** a decimal correct to 2 decimal places.

a $3\frac{2}{5} + 4\frac{7}{8} = ?$

The sum of $3\frac{2}{5}$ and $4\frac{7}{8}$ is $8\frac{11}{40}$.

b The sum of $3\frac{2}{5}$ and $4\frac{7}{8} \approx 8 \cdot 28$.

Press	Display
C	0
3 $a^{b}/_{c}$ 2 $a^{b}/_{c}$ 5	$3\frac{2}{5}$
+ 4 $a^{b}/_{c}$ 7 $a^{b}/_{c}$ 8	$4\frac{7}{8}$
=	$8\frac{11}{40}$

7 Find the sum of the following mixed numbers. Express your answer as a mixed number and as a decimal correct to 2 decimal places.

a $2\frac{7}{9} + 5\frac{3}{11}$

b $4\frac{6}{7} + 9\frac{7}{12}$

Let's Practise!

8 Add. Express your answer in its simplest form. Then check your answer with a calculator.

a $5\frac{5}{6} + 3\frac{5}{12}$

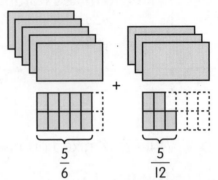

$\frac{5}{6}$ $\frac{5}{12}$

b $1\frac{1}{4} + 2\frac{2}{5}$

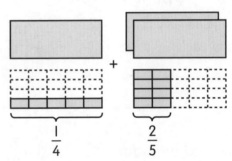

$\frac{1}{4}$ $\frac{2}{5}$

c $3\frac{3}{8} + 4\frac{1}{3}$

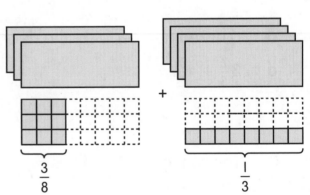

$\frac{3}{8}$ $\frac{1}{3}$

9 Find the sum of the mixed numbers. Express your answer as:

i a mixed number   **ii** a decimal correct to 2 decimal places.

a $1\frac{3}{5} + 2\frac{3}{8}$ **b** $3\frac{3}{4} + 5\frac{2}{7}$ **c** $5\frac{1}{6} + 2\frac{2}{9}$

Practice Book 5A, p.81

Let's Learn!

Subtracting mixed numbers

1 Tai bought $2\frac{3}{4}$ m of material. He cut $1\frac{1}{8}$ m to make a bag. How much material did he have left?

To subtract, change $\frac{1}{8}$ and $\frac{3}{4}$ to like fractions first.

$$\begin{array}{c} \overset{\times 2}{\frown} \\ \frac{3}{4} = \frac{6}{8} \\ \underset{\times 2}{\smile} \end{array}$$

$$2\frac{3}{4} - 1\frac{1}{8} = 2\frac{6}{8} - 1\frac{1}{8}$$
$$= 1\frac{5}{8}\text{m}$$

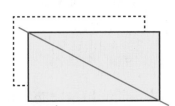
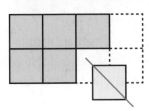

Tai had $1\frac{5}{8}$ m of material left.

2 Find the difference between $4\frac{5}{9}$ and $3\frac{5}{6}$.

$$4\frac{5}{9} - 3\frac{5}{6} = 4\frac{\boxed{}}{\boxed{}} - 3\frac{\boxed{}}{\boxed{}}$$

$$= \boxed{}\frac{\boxed{}}{\boxed{}} - \boxed{}\frac{\boxed{}}{\boxed{}}$$

$$= \frac{\boxed{}}{\boxed{}}$$

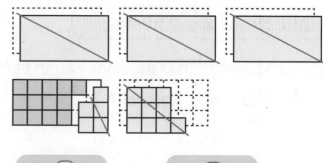

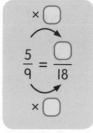

$$\frac{5}{9} = \frac{\boxed{}}{18}$$

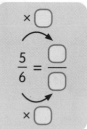

$$\frac{5}{6} = \frac{\boxed{}}{\boxed{}}$$

3 A bottle contained $3\frac{3}{8}\,\ell$ of water. Miya used $1\frac{1}{3}\,\ell$ of it. What was the volume of water left in the bottle?

$$3\frac{3}{8} - 1\frac{1}{3} = ?$$

 To subtract, change the fractional parts to like fractions first. Then subtract the whole numbers before subtracting the fractional parts.

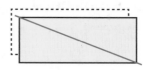 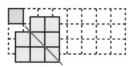

$$3\frac{3}{8} - 1\frac{1}{3} = 3\frac{9}{24} - 1\frac{8}{24}$$

$$= 2\frac{1}{24}\,\ell$$

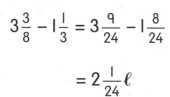

$$\frac{3}{8} \overset{\times 3}{=} \frac{9}{24} \quad (\times 3)$$

$$\frac{1}{3} \overset{\times 8}{=} \frac{8}{24} \quad (\times 8)$$

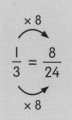

The volume of water left was $2\frac{1}{24}\,\ell$.

4 Subtract.

a $5\frac{5}{9} - 2\frac{1}{3} = 5\frac{\boxed{}}{9} - 2\frac{\boxed{}}{\boxed{}}$

$= \boxed{}\frac{\boxed{}}{\boxed{}}$

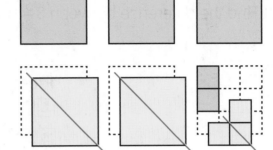
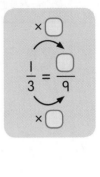

b $3\frac{4}{5} - 2\frac{1}{2} = \boxed{}\frac{\boxed{}}{\boxed{}} - \boxed{}\frac{\boxed{}}{\boxed{}}$

$= \boxed{}\frac{\boxed{}}{\boxed{}}$

Activity

5 Work in pairs.

The difference between two mixed numbers is $3\frac{1}{4}$. What are the two mixed numbers?

$$\boxed{}\frac{\boxed{}}{\boxed{}} - \boxed{}\frac{\boxed{}}{\boxed{}} = 3\frac{1}{4}$$

Activity

6 Find the difference between $3\frac{5}{8}$ and $1\frac{3}{5}$.

$$3\frac{5}{8} - 1\frac{3}{5} = ?$$

Press	Display
C	0
3 $a^{b}/_{c}$ 5 $a^{b}/_{c}$ 8	$3\frac{5}{8}$
– 1 $a^{b}/_{c}$ 3 $a^{b}/_{c}$ 5	$1\frac{3}{5}$
=	$2\frac{1}{40}$

The difference between $3\frac{5}{8}$ and $1\frac{3}{5}$ is $2\frac{1}{40}$.

7 Subtract. Express your answer as a mixed number and as a decimal. Correct the decimal to 2 decimal places if necessary.

a $5\frac{3}{11} - 4\frac{7}{8}$ **b** $9\frac{5}{12} - 3\frac{8}{9}$

Let's Practise!

8 Subtract without using a calculator. Then check your answer using a calculator.

a $3\frac{3}{4} - 1\frac{1}{2}$

Let's Practise!

b $5\frac{5}{6} - 2\frac{2}{3}$

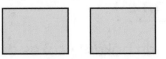

c $3\frac{1}{3} - 2\frac{1}{4}$

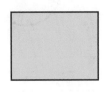 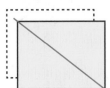

d $2\frac{3}{4} - 1\frac{3}{8}$

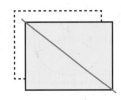 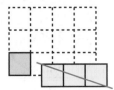

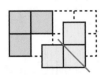

9 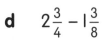 Subtract. Express your answer as a mixed number and a decimal. Correct the decimal to 2 decimal places if necessary.

a $6\frac{1}{10} - 3\frac{1}{5}$ **b** $4\frac{1}{2} - 1\frac{7}{8}$ **c** $5\frac{1}{4} - 2\frac{1}{3}$

d $7\frac{2}{3} - 4\frac{1}{2}$ **e** $9\frac{4}{7} - 2\frac{1}{3}$ **f** $12\frac{7}{12} - 5\frac{8}{9}$

Practice Book 5A, p.83

Let's Learn!

Word problems

1 Mr Newman baked 5 cakes of the same size. He divided the cakes equally into 3 portions. How many cakes were there in each portion?

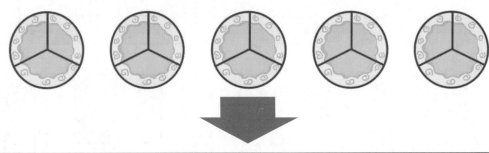

$5 \div 3 = \frac{5}{3} = 1\frac{2}{3}$ cakes

There were $1\frac{2}{3}$ cakes in each portion.

$$
\begin{array}{r}
1 \\
3{\overline{)\,5}} \\
-3 \\
\hline
2
\end{array}
$$

2 Alisha had 17 ℓ of fruit juice. She gave 5 ℓ of fruit juice to her sister. The remaining fruit juice was poured equally into 5 bottles. How much fruit juice did each bottle contain?

$17 - 5 = \boxed{}$ ℓ

She had $\boxed{}$ ℓ of fruit juice left.

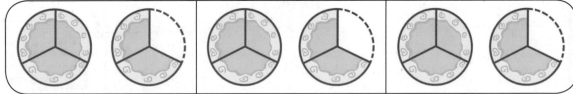

Each bottle contained $\boxed{}\dfrac{\boxed{}}{\boxed{}}$ ℓ of fruit juice.

3 Hardeep was given $\frac{4}{5}$h to complete his homework. He completed it in $\frac{3}{4}$h. How much spare time did he have left after he completed his homework?

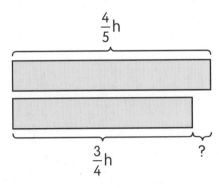

$$\frac{4}{5} - \frac{3}{4} = \frac{16}{20} - \frac{15}{20} = \frac{1}{20}h$$

Hardeep had $\frac{1}{20}$h left after he completed his homework.

4 Isabel spent $\frac{1}{6}$ of her money on food. She also spent $\frac{5}{8}$ of her money on a present. What fraction of Isabel's money was left?

$$\frac{\square}{\square} = \frac{\square}{\square} \qquad \frac{\square}{\square} = \frac{\square}{\square}$$

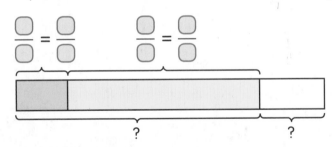

First find the amount of money Isabel spent on the food and present altogether.

$$\frac{\square}{\square} + \frac{\square}{\square} = \frac{\square}{\square}$$

Isabel spent $\frac{\square}{\square}$ of her money on the food and present altogether.

$$\square - \frac{\square}{\square} = \frac{\square}{\square}$$

$\frac{\square}{\square}$ of Isabel's money was left.

97

5 Lisa bought $1\frac{2}{9}\ell$ of orange squash. Ravi gave Lisa another $2\frac{1}{6}\ell$ of orange squash. How many litres of orange squash did Lisa have altogether?

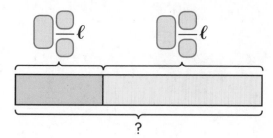

Lisa had ⬜⬜ ℓ of orange squash altogether.

6 Claire took $2\frac{1}{4}$h to finish reading a book. Her brother, Dan, took $\frac{2}{3}$h less to finish reading his book. How long did they spend to finish reading their books altogether?

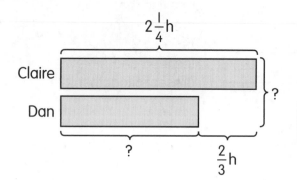

First find the time Dan took to read the book.

$2\frac{1}{4} - \frac{2}{3} = $ ⬜⬜ h

Dan finished reading his book in $1\frac{7}{12}$h.

$2\frac{1}{4} + 1\frac{7}{12} = $ ⬜⬜ h

Claire and Dan spent ⬜⬜ h to finish reading their books altogether.

Let's Practise!

Solve these word problems. Show your workings clearly.

7 Ethan had 5 bags of green beans, each with a mass of 7 kg. He divided all the beans equally into 3 portions. What was the mass of the beans in each portion?

8 Rosa cuts a 15 m length of the string into 4 equal pieces. What is the length of each piece of string?

9 Sian spent $\frac{1}{4}$ of her money on Monday and $\frac{7}{10}$ of it on Tuesday. What fraction of Sian's money was spent during the two days?

Solve these word problems. You can use your calculator in this section.

10 Serge runs $1\frac{7}{8}$ km. Sam runs $\frac{1}{2}$ km less than Serge. How many kilometres does Sam run?

11 George drank $1\frac{5}{9}\ell$ of water per day. Harry drank $\frac{5}{12}\ell$ of water less than George per day. How many litres of water did Harry drink per day?

12 Sophie bought $2\frac{5}{6}$ kg of flour. Ali bought $\frac{5}{9}$ kg more flour than Sophie. How many kilograms of flour did Ali buy?

13 Mr Lee poured out $2\frac{1}{2}\ell$ of apple juice. He gave $\frac{7}{8}\ell$ of the juice to Selina and $\frac{5}{12}\ell$ to Rosalind. How many litres of apple juice did Mr Lee have left?

14 Mr Taylor sold $5\frac{2}{3}$ kg of sugar in the morning. He sold $\frac{11}{12}$ kg less sugar in the afternoon. How many kilograms of sugar did Mr Taylor sell in the morning and afternoon altogether?

Practice Book 5A, p.85 and p.89

Maths Journal

15 Sarah, Ava and Hannah worked out the following:

$$\frac{5}{6} + \frac{7}{9} = ?$$

Sarah's answer: $\frac{12}{15}$ Ava's answer: $2\frac{9}{18}$ Hannah's answer: $1\frac{11}{18}$

Two of the three answers are incorrect.

a   Whose answers are incorrect?

b   Explain why.

Let's Wrap It Up!

You have learnt to:

- identify like fractions, which have the same denominator
- identify unlike fractions, which have different denominators
- add and subtract unlike fractions by converting them to like fractions
- express division as a fraction and vice versa
- convert proper fractions, improper fractions and mixed numbers to decimals by:
  (a)   converting to tenths, hundredths and thousandths
  (b)   using long division
  (c)   using a calculator
- add and subtract mixed numbers using a calculator.

Let's Revise!

Anna took $1\frac{2}{5}$ h to paint a cupboard and $1\frac{2}{3}$ h to paint a bookshelf.

Jacob took $\frac{2}{3}$ h less than Anna to paint a similar cupboard and bookshelf.

Let's Wrap It Up!

a How long did Anna take to paint both the cupboard and bookshelf?

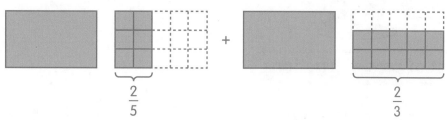

$\frac{2}{5}$ + $\frac{2}{3}$

$1\frac{2}{5} + 1\frac{2}{3} = 2\frac{16}{15} = 3\frac{1}{15}$ h

Anna took $3\frac{1}{15}$ h to paint the cupboard and bookshelf.

b How long did Jacob spend to paint a similar cupboard and bookshelf?

  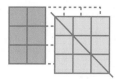 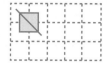

$3\frac{1}{15} - \frac{2}{3} = 2\frac{6}{15} = 2\frac{2}{5}$ h

Jacob took $2\frac{2}{5}$ h to paint a similar cupboard and bookshelf.

Put On Your Thinking Caps!

16 Jack had two identical bottles. The first bottle contained 1ℓ of water.
The second bottle contained $\frac{5}{9}\ell$ of water.
What amount of water must Jack pour from the first bottle into the
second bottle so that both bottles contain the same amount of water?
Express your answer as a fraction.

Practice Book 5A, p.94

4 Fractions (2)

Let's Learn!

> **Product of proper fractions**

1 Ella draws a rectangle and colours $\frac{3}{5}$ of it blue.

She then draws red stripes over $\frac{1}{2}$ of the coloured parts.

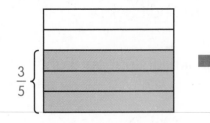

$$\frac{1}{2} \text{ of } \frac{3}{5} = \frac{1}{2} \times \frac{3}{5}$$

$$= \frac{1 \times 3}{2 \times 5}$$

$$= \frac{3}{10}$$

$\frac{1}{2}$ of $\frac{3}{5}$

Jack draws an identical rectangle and colours $\frac{1}{2}$ of it blue.

He then draws red stripes over $\frac{3}{5}$ of the coloured parts.

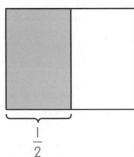

$\frac{1}{2}$

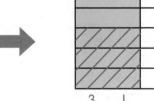

$\frac{3}{5}$ of $\frac{1}{2}$

$$\frac{3}{5} \text{ of } \frac{1}{2} = \frac{3}{5} \times \frac{1}{2}$$

$$= \frac{3 \times 1}{5 \times 2}$$

$$= \frac{3}{10}$$

Do Ella and Jack get the same answer?

We say $\frac{1}{2}$ of $\frac{3}{5}$ ◯ $\frac{3}{5}$ of $\frac{1}{2}$.

There are ⬭ parts in each of Ella's and Jack's rectangles.
⬭ coloured parts in each rectangle have red stripes.

$\frac{⬭}{⬭}$ of each rectangle has red stripes.

2 Find the product.

Method I

$$\frac{3}{4} \times \frac{8}{9} = \frac{3 \times 8}{4 \times 9}$$

$$= \frac{24}{36}$$

$$= \frac{2}{3}$$

Method 2

$$\frac{3}{4} \times \frac{8}{9} = \frac{\overset{1}{\cancel{3}}}{4} \times \frac{8}{\underset{3}{\cancel{9}}} \longleftarrow$$ Divide both the numerator and denominator by the common factor, 3.

$$= \frac{\overset{1}{\cancel{3}}{}^{1}}{\underset{1}{\cancel{4}}} \times \frac{\overset{2}{\cancel{8}}{}^{2}}{\underset{3}{\cancel{9}}} \longleftarrow$$ Divide both the numerator and denominator by the common factor, 4.

$$= \frac{1 \times 2}{1 \times 3}$$

$$= \frac{2}{3}$$

3 Find the product.

a $\frac{3}{10}$ of $\frac{5}{9} = \dfrac{\bigcirc}{\bigcirc}$

b $\frac{4}{10} \times \frac{5}{12} = \dfrac{\bigcirc}{\bigcirc}$

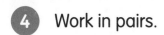

Activity

4   Work in pairs.

Each group will need a sheet of grid paper.

I   Draw a rectangle on the grid paper.

2   Divide the rectangle into 4 equal parts. Colour $\frac{3}{4}$ of it.

3   Draw crosses on $\frac{1}{4}$ of the coloured parts.

How many coloured parts have crosses on them?

How many parts are there altogether?

What fraction of the whole rectangle has crosses on it?

$\frac{1}{4}$ of $\frac{3}{4} = \dfrac{\bigcirc}{\bigcirc}$

4   Now draw a rectangle identical to the first one.

5   Colour $\frac{1}{4}$ of it.

Activity

6 Draw crosses on $\frac{3}{4}$ of the coloured parts.

How many coloured parts have crosses on them?

How many parts are there altogether?

What fraction of the whole rectangle has crosses on it?

$$\frac{3}{4} \text{ of } \frac{1}{4} = \frac{\bigcirc}{\bigcirc}$$

Do you get the same answer in both cases?

What can you say about $\frac{1}{4}$ of $\frac{3}{4}$ and $\frac{3}{4}$ of $\frac{1}{4}$?

Let's Explore!

5 Find the product of the following whole numbers.

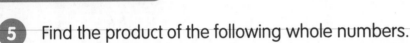

$3 \times 4 = \boxed{}$ $5 \times 17 = \boxed{}$ $9 \times 8 = \boxed{}$ $12 \times 7 = \boxed{}$

What do you notice about each product?
Is it greater than each of the whole numbers used to find the product?
Explain why.

Next find the product of the following fractions.

$\frac{1}{2} \times \frac{3}{4} = \boxed{}$ $\frac{3}{4} \times \frac{4}{5} = \boxed{}$ $\frac{2}{7} \times \frac{3}{4} = \boxed{}$ $\frac{1}{6} \times \frac{5}{9} = \boxed{}$

What do you notice about each product?
Is it greater than each of the fractions used to find the product?
Explain why.

Let's Practise!

6 Find the value of each product in its simplest form.

a $\frac{7}{10}$ of $\frac{5}{10}$ **b** $\frac{3}{8}$ of $\frac{4}{6}$ **c** $\frac{1}{3} \times \frac{6}{7}$ **d** $\frac{6}{8} \times \frac{4}{9}$

Practice Book 5A, p.95

Let's Learn!

Word problems (I)

1 Peter had $\frac{3}{4}\ell$ of vegetable stock. He used $\frac{2}{3}$ of it to make some soup.

a How much vegetable stock did he use to make the soup?

b How much vegetable stock did he have left?

Method I

4 units ⟶ 1ℓ

I unit ⟶ $\frac{1}{4}\ell$

2 units ⟶ $\frac{1}{2}\ell$

The model above shows that:

a Peter used $\frac{1}{2}\ell$ of vegetable stock to make the soup.

b He had $\frac{1}{4}\ell$ of vegetable stock left.

Method 2

a $\dfrac{\overset{1}{\cancel{2}}}{\underset{1}{\cancel{3}}} \times \dfrac{\overset{1}{\cancel{3}}}{\underset{2}{\cancel{4}}} = \dfrac{1}{2}\ell$

Peter used $\frac{1}{2}\ell$ of vegetable stock to make the soup.

b $\dfrac{3}{4} - \dfrac{1}{2} = \dfrac{3}{4} - \dfrac{2}{4}$

$= \dfrac{1}{4}\ell$

He had $\frac{1}{4}\ell$ of vegetable stock left.

2 Farha bought $\frac{4}{5}$ kg of sugar. She used $\frac{3}{4}$ of it to make some cakes.

a How much sugar did she use?

b How much sugar was left?

Method I

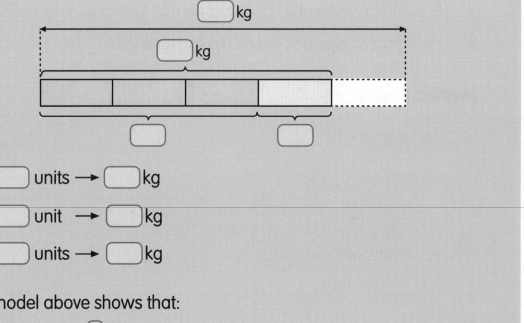

⬚ units ⟶ ⬚ kg

⬚ unit ⟶ ⬚ kg

⬚ units ⟶ ⬚ kg

The model above shows that:

a Farha used $\frac{\Box}{\Box}$ kg of sugar.

b $\frac{\Box}{\Box}$ kg of sugar was left.

Method 2

a $\frac{3}{4} \times \frac{\Box}{\Box} = \frac{\Box}{\Box}$ kg

Farha used $\frac{\Box}{\Box}$ kg of sugar.

b $\frac{4}{5} - \frac{\Box}{\Box} = \frac{\Box}{\Box}$ kg

$\frac{\Box}{\Box}$ kg of sugar was left.

3 Miya had a sum of money. She saved $\frac{1}{4}$ of it. She spent $\frac{4}{9}$ of the remainder on a football.

a What fraction of her money was spent on the football?

b What fraction of her money was left?

Method I

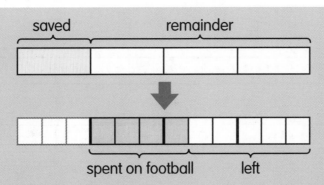

saved · remainder

spent on football · left

The model above shows that:
Number of units spent on football = 4
Number of units left = 5
Total number of units in I whole = 12

a Fraction of money spent on football = $\frac{4}{12}$ = $\frac{1}{3}$

$\frac{1}{3}$ of her money was spent on the football.

b $\frac{5}{12}$ of her money was left.

Method 2

a $1 - \frac{1}{4} = \frac{3}{4}$ (remainder)

$\frac{\overset{1}{\cancel{4}}}{\underset{3}{\cancel{9}}} \times \frac{\overset{1}{\cancel{3}}}{\underset{1}{\cancel{4}}} = \frac{1}{3}$

$\frac{1}{3}$ of her money was spent on the football.

b $\frac{3}{4} - \frac{1}{3} = \frac{9}{12} - \frac{4}{12}$

$= \frac{5}{12}$

$\frac{5}{12}$ of her money was left.

4 Hardeep cut $\frac{3}{5}$ of a pie for his friends. He gave $\frac{3}{4}$ of the remainder to his brother.

a What fraction of the pie did he give to his brother?

b What fraction of the pie did he have left?

Method I

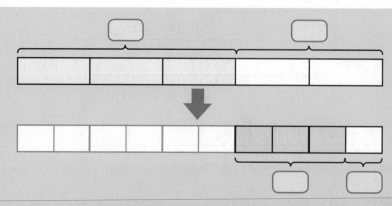

The model above shows that:

Number of units given to Hardeep's brother = ☐

Total number of units in I whole = ☐

a He gave $\dfrac{\boxed{}}{\boxed{}}$ of the pie to his brother.

b He had $\dfrac{\boxed{}}{\boxed{}}$ of the pie left.

Method 2

a $1 - \dfrac{\boxed{}}{\boxed{}} = \dfrac{\boxed{}}{\boxed{}}$ (remainder)

$\dfrac{3}{4} \times \dfrac{\boxed{}}{\boxed{}} = \dfrac{\boxed{}}{\boxed{}}$

He gave $\dfrac{\boxed{}}{\boxed{}}$ of the pie to his brother.

b $1 - \dfrac{\boxed{}}{\boxed{}} - \dfrac{\boxed{}}{\boxed{}} = \dfrac{\boxed{}}{\boxed{}}$

He had $\dfrac{\boxed{}}{\boxed{}}$ of the pie left.

Let's Practise!

Solve these word problems. Draw models to help you where necessary.

5 Mrs Smith had a plot of land. She planted flowering plants on $\frac{3}{4}$ of the land. $\frac{2}{3}$ of the flowering plants were sunflowers. What fraction of the land was planted with sunflowers?

6 Matt spent $\frac{7}{9}$ of his time in the morning studying French and English. He spent $\frac{4}{7}$ of this time studying French. What fraction of the total time did he spend studying English?

7 Ruby has a piece of string $\frac{5}{6}$ m in length. She cuts $\frac{3}{5}$ of it to tie some papers together. What is the length of string left?

8 A farmer sold $\frac{7}{12}$ of his animals. Of his remaining animals, $\frac{3}{5}$ were chickens and the rest were ducks. What fraction of all the animals were the unsold ducks?

9 Michael ate $\frac{1}{6}$ of a cake. He gave $\frac{1}{5}$ of the remainder to his friend. He kept the rest of the cake. What fraction of the cake did he keep?

10 Mrs Lim used $\frac{1}{3}$ of a pack of butter to make some biscuits. Then she used $\frac{5}{8}$ of the remaining butter to make some tarts. What fraction of the butter was left?

11 Lisa spent $\frac{2}{5}$ of her money on a jacket. She then spent $\frac{4}{9}$ of her remaining money on a pair of shoes. What fraction of her money was left?

Practice Book 5A, p.97

Let's Learn!

> ### Product of an improper fraction and a proper or improper fraction

1 Find the product of $\frac{6}{5}$ and $\frac{3}{4}$.

$\frac{6}{5} \times \frac{3}{4}$

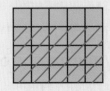 

$$\frac{6}{5} \times \frac{3}{4} = \frac{\cancel{6}^{3}}{5} \times \frac{3}{\cancel{4}_{2}}$$

$$= \frac{3 \times 3}{5 \times 2}$$

$$= \frac{9}{10}$$

$\frac{18}{20} = \frac{9}{10}$

We can also find the answer using a calculator.

Press	Display
C	0
6 $a^{b/c}$ 5	$\frac{6}{5}$
× 3 $a^{b/c}$ 4	$\frac{3}{4}$
=	$\frac{9}{10}$

2 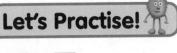 Find the product.

a $\dfrac{2}{7} \times \dfrac{21}{12}$

b $\dfrac{16}{3} \times \dfrac{9}{4}$

c $\dfrac{3}{7} \times \dfrac{14}{5}$

d $\dfrac{7}{6} \times \dfrac{3}{11}$

e $\dfrac{9}{4} \times \dfrac{10}{3}$

f $\dfrac{7}{5} \times \dfrac{9}{2}$

Let's Practise!

3 Find the product.

a $\dfrac{1}{3} \times \dfrac{7}{5}$

b $\dfrac{15}{6} \times \dfrac{4}{5}$

c $\dfrac{21}{8} \times \dfrac{10}{7}$

d $\dfrac{32}{12} \times \dfrac{15}{4}$

e $\dfrac{17}{3} \times \dfrac{22}{5}$

f $\dfrac{14}{9} \times \dfrac{11}{3}$

g $\dfrac{28}{11} \times \dfrac{43}{12}$

h $\dfrac{23}{13} \times \dfrac{11}{3}$

Practice Book 5A, p.103

Let's Learn!

Product of a mixed number and a whole number

1 There are 6 children in the Walker family. Each child is given $1\frac{1}{2}$ sandwiches. How many sandwiches did they get altogether?

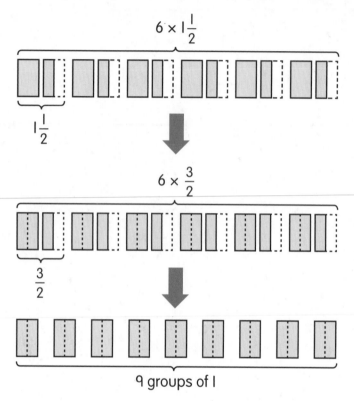

$6 \times 1\frac{1}{2}$

$1\frac{1}{2}$

$6 \times \frac{3}{2}$

$\frac{3}{2}$

9 groups of 1

Press		Display
C		0
1 $a^b/_c$ 1 $a^b/_c$ 2		$1\frac{1}{2}$
× 6		6
=		9

$1\frac{1}{2} = \frac{3}{2}$

$1\frac{1}{2} \times 6$ is the same

as 6 groups of $1\frac{1}{2}$.

Use a calculator to find the product.

They got 9 sandwiches altogether.

2 Find the product of $2\frac{1}{3}$ and 5.

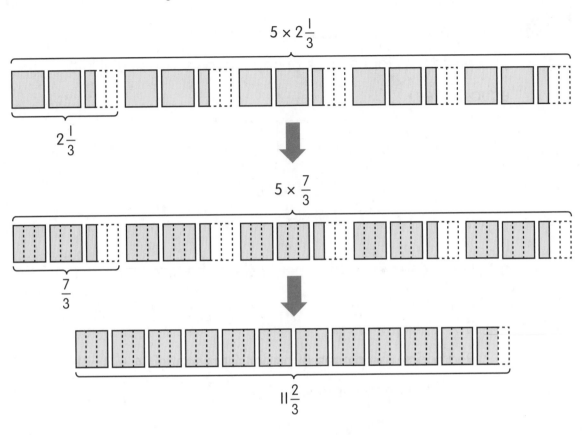

$5 \times 2\frac{1}{3}$

$2\frac{1}{3}$

$5 \times \frac{7}{3}$

$\frac{7}{3}$

$11\frac{2}{3}$

$2\frac{1}{3} \times 5 = \dfrac{\bigcirc}{\bigcirc} \times 5$

$\qquad = \dfrac{\bigcirc}{\bigcirc}$

$\qquad = \dfrac{33}{3} + \dfrac{\bigcirc}{\bigcirc}$

$\qquad = 11 + \dfrac{\bigcirc}{\bigcirc}$

$\qquad = \bigcirc\dfrac{\bigcirc}{\bigcirc}$

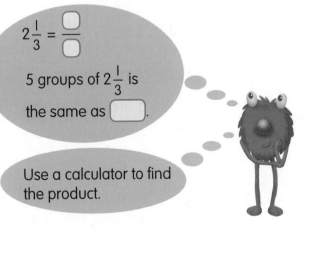

$2\frac{1}{3} = \dfrac{\bigcirc}{\bigcirc}$

5 groups of $2\frac{1}{3}$ is the same as $\boxed{}$.

Use a calculator to find the product.

Activity

3 You will need some pieces of paper that represent I whole.

To represent $\frac{1}{2}$, fold a piece of paper into two and cut it into equal halves.

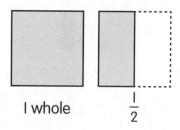

I whole $\frac{1}{2}$

a Use these pieces of paper to show the following:

 i $3\frac{1}{2}$ **ii** $4 \times 3\frac{1}{2}$ **iii** $3\frac{1}{2} \times 5$

b Rearrange the pieces of paper representing $4 \times 3\frac{1}{2}$. How many wholes are there in $4 \times 3\frac{1}{2}$?

4 ▢ ▢ ▢ ▢ ▯

Look at this diagram showing $4\frac{1}{2}$.

Express this as a product of another mixed number and a whole number.

$$4\frac{1}{2} = \boxed{}\frac{\boxed{}}{\boxed{}} \times 2$$

$2 \times \boxed{} = 4$

$2 \times \dfrac{\boxed{}}{\boxed{}} = \dfrac{1}{2}$

Use the same method to find the missing number below.

$$8\frac{1}{4} = \boxed{}\frac{\boxed{}}{\boxed{}} \times 2$$

Let's Practise!

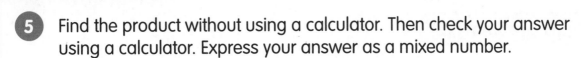

5 Find the product without using a calculator. Then check your answer using a calculator. Express your answer as a mixed number.

a $1\frac{1}{2} \times 3 = $ ☐ ☐/☐

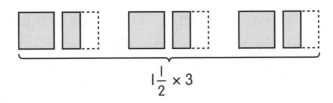

$$1\frac{1}{2} \times 3$$

b $2\frac{1}{3} \times 2 = $ ☐ ☐/☐

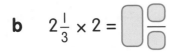

$$2\frac{1}{3} \times 2$$

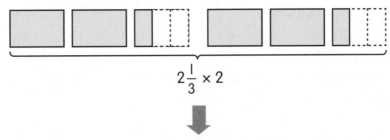

6 🖩 Find the product. Express your answer as a whole number or a mixed number.

a $3\frac{9}{11} \times 33$ **b** $14 \times 2\frac{3}{5}$ **c** $38 \times 5\frac{2}{7}$

Practice Book 5A, p.105

Let's Learn!

Word problems (2)

You can use your calculator in this section.

1 During an art class, Miss Brook asked her pupils to cut out $1\frac{1}{2}$ circles each from pieces of paper. There were 24 pupils in the class altogether. Miss Brook then arranged the cut-outs to make whole circles. How many whole circles were there?

1 pupil $\longrightarrow 1\frac{1}{2}$ circles

24 pupils $\longrightarrow 24 \times 1\frac{1}{2}$

$= 36$ circles

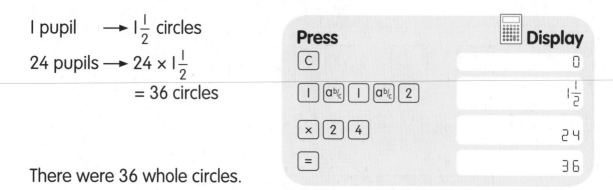

Press	Display
C	0
1 aᵇ/c 1 aᵇ/c 2	$1\frac{1}{2}$
× 2 4	2 4
=	3 6

There were 36 whole circles.

2 There were 40 guests at a party. Each guest ate $2\frac{3}{4}$ mini pizzas. How many mini pizzas did the guests eat altogether?

1 guest $\longrightarrow 2\frac{3}{4}$ mini pizzas

40 guests $\longrightarrow$ ☐ $\times 2\frac{3}{4}$

$=$ ☐ mini pizzas

You can use a calculator to find the answer.

The guests ate ☐ mini pizzas altogether.

3 An allotment plot has a length of $12\frac{3}{4}$ m and a width of 7 m.
Find the area of this plot. Express your answer as a decimal.

Area of plot = length × width

= ⬭ × ⬭

= ⬭ m²

4 Lucy bought 4 bags of potatoes. The mass of each bag of potatoes was
$2\frac{3}{5}$ kg. Each kilogram of potatoes cost £2. How much did Lucy pay for the
4 bags of potatoes?

1 bag of potatoes ⟶ $2\frac{3}{5}$ kg

4 bags of potatoes ⟶ $4 \times 2\frac{3}{5}$

$= 10\frac{2}{5}$ kg

The mass of 4 bags of potatoes was $10\frac{2}{5}$ kg.

1 kg of potatoes ⟶ £2

$10\frac{2}{5}$ kg of potatoes ⟶ $10\frac{2}{5} \times$ £2

= £20·80

Lucy paid £20·80 for the 4 bags of potatoes.

5   Tom used 3 bottles of syrup to make some desserts. Each bottle contained $1\frac{1}{2}\,\ell$ of syrup. The cost of $1\,\ell$ of syrup was £5. Find the total cost of the syrup he used.

I bottle   ⟶ ☐ ℓ

3 bottles ⟶ 3 × ☐ ℓ

= ☐ ℓ

3 bottles contained ☐ ℓ of syrup.

$1\,\ell$ of syrup   ⟶ £5

☐ ℓ of syrup ⟶ ☐ × £5

= £ ☐

The total cost of the syrup he used was £ ☐.

Let's Practise!

Solve these word problems. Show your workings clearly.

6   Ben has 6 children. He gives each child $2\frac{1}{3}$ sandwiches. How many sandwiches does he need?

7   Amy cuts a ball of string into 15 equal pieces. The length of each piece of string is $15\frac{1}{4}$ cm. What is the total length of the string?

8   Mr Peters buys 9 packs of meat. Each pack of meat weighs $7\frac{1}{2}$ kg. The cost of 1 kg of meat is £3. How much does he pay for all the meat he buys?

9   Miss Owen bought a plot of land 12 m long and $5\frac{2}{5}$ m wide. The cost of 1 m² of land is £2200. How much did Miss Owen pay for the whole plot of land?

Practice Book 5A, p.107

Let's Learn!

Dividing a fraction by a whole number

1 Half of a cottage pie is shared equally among 3 children. What fraction of the cottage pie will each child get?

Method 1

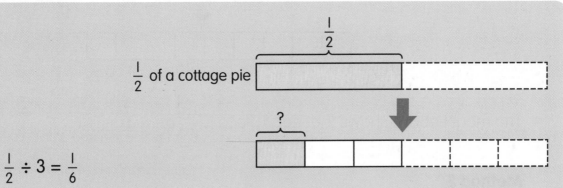

$\frac{1}{2} \div 3 = \frac{1}{6}$

The model above shows that each child will get $\frac{1}{6}$ of the cottage pie.

Method 2

$\frac{1}{2} \div 3 = \frac{1}{3}$ of $\frac{1}{2}$

$\qquad = \frac{1}{3} \times \frac{1}{2}$

$\qquad = \frac{1}{6}$

Each child will get
$\frac{1}{3}$ of $\frac{1}{2}$ of the cottage pie.

Each child will get $\frac{1}{6}$ of the cottage pie.

Method 3

$\frac{1}{2} \div 3 = \frac{1}{2} \times \frac{1}{3}$

$\qquad = \frac{1}{6}$

Multiply $\frac{1}{2}$ by $\frac{1}{3}$.

Each child will get $\frac{1}{6}$ of the cottage pie.

2 A coil of wire, $\frac{3}{5}$m long, is cut into 6 equal pieces. How long is each piece of the wire?

Method 1

$\frac{3}{5} \div 6 = \frac{\square}{\square}$m

1m

$\frac{3}{5}$m

?

The model above shows that each piece is $\frac{\square}{\square}$m.

Method 2

$\frac{3}{5} \div 6 = \frac{1}{6}$ of $\frac{3}{5}$

$= \frac{\square}{\square} \times \frac{\square}{\square}$

$= \frac{\square}{\square}$m

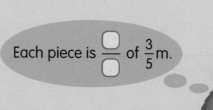

Each piece is $\frac{\square}{\square}$ of $\frac{3}{5}$m.

Each piece is $\frac{\square}{\square}$m.

Method 3

$\frac{3}{5} \div 6 = \frac{3}{5} \times \frac{\square}{\square}$

$= \frac{\square}{\square}$m

Each piece is $\frac{\square}{\square}$m.

3 A watermelon with a mass of $\frac{4}{7}$ kg is cut into 2 equal pieces. What is the mass of each piece of watermelon?

Method I

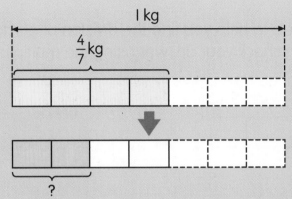

The model above shows that the mass of each piece of watermelon is $\frac{2}{7}$ kg.

Method 2

$\frac{4}{7} \div 2 = \frac{4}{7} \times \frac{1}{2}$

$\qquad = \frac{2}{7}$ kg

The mass of each piece of watermelon is $\frac{2}{7}$ kg.

4 Find the value of $\frac{9}{11} \div 3$.

Method I

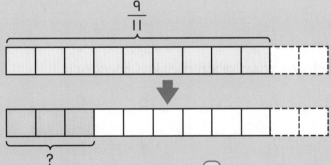

The model above shows that $\frac{9}{11} \div 3 = \dfrac{\bigcirc}{\bigcirc}$

Method 2

$\frac{9}{11} \div 3 = \frac{9}{11} \times \dfrac{\bigcirc}{\bigcirc}$

$\qquad = \dfrac{\bigcirc}{\bigcirc}$

Activity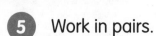

5 Work in pairs.

Use the models to help you find the division of a fraction by a whole number. Then check your answer using the multiplication method.

a Divide $\frac{1}{4}$ by 3.

b Divide $\frac{1}{3}$ by 5.

Check: $\frac{1}{4} \div 3 = \dfrac{\square}{\square}$ of $\dfrac{\square}{\square}$

$= \dfrac{\square}{\square} \times \dfrac{\square}{\square}$

$= \dfrac{\square}{\square}$

Let's Practise!

6 Divide.

a $\frac{2}{7} \div 4 = \frac{2}{7} \times \frac{1}{4}$

   $= \dfrac{\square}{\square}$

b $\frac{2}{3} \div 8 = \frac{2}{3} \times \frac{1}{8}$

   $= \dfrac{\square}{\square}$

c $\frac{3}{4} \div 12$

d $\frac{6}{7} \div 9$

7 Draw a model to solve each division sentence.

a $\frac{6}{11} \div 3$

b $\frac{8}{9} \div 4$

c $\frac{2}{5} \div 4$

d $\frac{3}{7} \div 2$

8 Solve these word problems. Draw models to help you where necessary.

a A box contained red and green apples. $\frac{4}{5}$ of the apples were red. The red apples were shared equally among 8 children. What fraction of all the apples from the box did each child get?

Let's Practise!

b Hardeep cut out $\frac{9}{10}$ of a cake. This portion of the cake was shared equally among Tai, Miya and Omar. What fraction of the cake did each of them get?

c The area of a rectangular piece of material is $\frac{4}{9}$ m². Julie cuts the material into 3 smaller pieces of the same size. What is the area of each small piece of material?

d A plank of wood $\frac{3}{5}$ m long is cut into 4 pieces of the same length. Find the length of each piece of wood.

e Mrs Ford gave $\frac{1}{3}$ of her savings to Lisa and $\frac{5}{12}$ of her savings to James. Then she deposited the rest of her savings equally in 3 accounts. What fraction of her savings did she put in each account?

f Sophia bought $\frac{3}{8}$ ℓ of blackcurrant squash. She poured the squash equally into 6 identical cups. Find the amount of squash in litres:

i in each cup

ii in 5 cups.

g Christine bought $\frac{5}{9}$ kg of mixed spice. She repacked it equally into 15 packets.

i Find the mass of 1 packet of mixed spice in kilograms.

ii She sold 7 packets of mixed spice. How many kilograms of mixed spice did she sell?

Practice Book 5A, p.109

Let's Learn!

Word problems (3)

1 Ron had 240 apples. He sold $\frac{1}{2}$ of them to Chris and $\frac{1}{3}$ to Jenny.

    a How many apples did Ron sell altogether?

    b How many apples did he have left?

$\frac{1}{2}$ of 6 units = $\frac{1}{2}$ × 6

                  = 3 units

$\frac{1}{3}$ of 6 units = $\frac{1}{3}$ × 6

                  = 2 units

Method 1

6 is a common multiple of 2 and 3.
Draw a model with 6 equal units.

240 apples

$\frac{1}{2}$ $\frac{1}{3}$ left

The model above shows that:

6 units → 240 apples

1 unit → 240 ÷ 6 = ☐ apples

5 units → 5 × ☐ = 200 apples

    a Ron sold 200 apples.   **b** He had 40 apples left.

Method 2

$\frac{1}{2} = \frac{3}{6}$ $\frac{1}{3} = \frac{2}{6}$

Fraction of apples sold is $\frac{3}{6} + \frac{2}{6} = \frac{5}{6}$.

$\frac{5}{6}$ of 240 = $\frac{5}{6}$ × 240 = 200 apples

    a Ron sold 200 apples.

    b He had 240 − 200

         = 40 apples left.

Method 3

$\frac{1}{2}$ × 240 = 120

$\frac{1}{3}$ × 240 = 80

    a Ron sold 120 + 80 = 200 apples.

    b He had 240 − 200

         = 40 apples left.

2 Kim planted 312 carrots, tomatoes, and pumpkins in her garden. $\frac{2}{3}$ of her plants were carrots and $\frac{1}{4}$ of them were tomatoes. The rest of the plants were pumpkins. How many pumpkins did she plant?

Method I

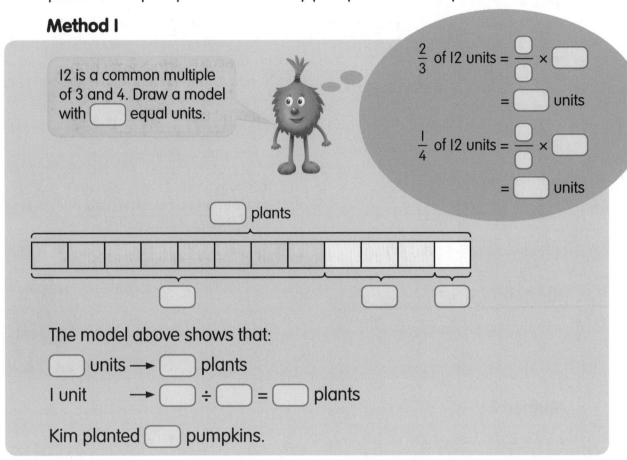

12 is a common multiple of 3 and 4. Draw a model with ☐ equal units.

$\frac{2}{3}$ of 12 units = $\dfrac{\bigcirc}{\bigcirc}$ × ☐

= ☐ units

$\frac{1}{4}$ of 12 units = $\dfrac{\bigcirc}{\bigcirc}$ × ☐

= ☐ units

☐ plants

☐   ☐   ☐

The model above shows that:

☐ units ⟶ ☐ plants

I unit ⟶ ☐ ÷ ☐ = ☐ plants

Kim planted ☐ pumpkins.

Method 2

$\frac{2}{3}$ = $\dfrac{\bigcirc}{\bigcirc}$ $\frac{1}{4}$ = $\dfrac{\bigcirc}{\bigcirc}$

I − $\dfrac{\bigcirc}{\bigcirc}$ − $\dfrac{\bigcirc}{\bigcirc}$ = $\dfrac{\bigcirc}{\bigcirc}$

$\dfrac{\bigcirc}{\bigcirc}$ of 312 = $\dfrac{\bigcirc}{\bigcirc}$ × 312

= ☐ pumpkins

Kim planted ☐ pumpkins.

3 Mrs Barlow had £480. She used $\frac{1}{3}$ of it to buy a game console. Then she spent $\frac{1}{4}$ of the remainder on some games. How much money did she have left?

Method I

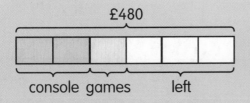

£480

console games   left

First draw a model with 3 parts. Shade I part to show the amount spent on the console.

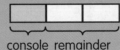

console remainder

The model above shows that:

6 units ⟶ £480

I unit ⟶ £$\frac{480}{6}$ = £80

3 units ⟶ 3 × £80 = £240

She had £240 left.

Then divide the model further to show I part of the remainder is spent on the games.

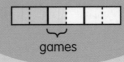

games

Method 2

$\frac{1}{3}$ of £480 = $\frac{1}{3}$ × £480

= £160

Mrs Barlow spent £160 on the console.

£480 – £160 = £320
After buying the console, she had £320 left.

$1 - \frac{1}{4} = \frac{3}{4}$

$\frac{3}{4}$ of £320 = $\frac{3}{4}$ × £320

= £240

She had £240 left.

4 In a test consisting of Sections A, B and C, Peter spent $\frac{1}{5}$ of his time on Section A, $\frac{1}{3}$ of the remaining time on Section B and the rest of the time on Section C. If he spent 48 minutes on Section C, how much time did he take to complete the whole test?

Method I

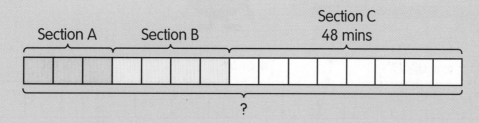

The model above shows that:

8 units → 48 mins

1 unit → 6 mins

15 units → 90 mins

Peter took 90 mins to complete the test.

Method 2

$\frac{1}{3} \times \frac{4}{5} = \frac{4}{15}$ (Section B)

$\frac{1}{5} + \frac{4}{15} = \frac{3}{15} + \frac{4}{15} = \frac{7}{15}$ (Sections A & B)

$1 - \frac{7}{15} = \frac{8}{15}$ (Section C)

$\frac{8}{15}$ → 48 mins

$\frac{15}{15}$ → 90 mins

Peter took 90 mins to complete the test.

5 Tim prepared a mixture of apple, carrot and orange juice. $\frac{1}{3}$ of the mixture was apple juice and $\frac{2}{5}$ of the remainder was orange juice. 315 ml of the mixture was orange juice. What volume of the mixture was carrot juice?

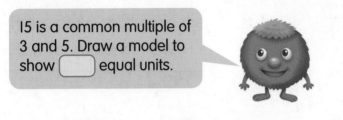

15 is a common multiple of 3 and 5. Draw a model to show ☐ equal units.

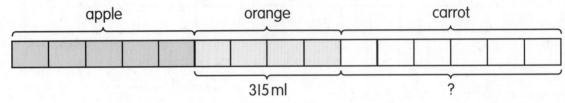

apple   orange   carrot

315 ml   ?

The model above shows that:

4 units ⟶ 315 ml

1 unit ⟶ 315 ÷ 4 = ☐ ml

6 units ⟶ 6 × ☐ = ☐ ml

☐ ml of the mixture was carrot juice.

6 Nick gave his cousin $\frac{1}{3}$ of his plastic bricks. He gave his sister $\frac{5}{6}$ of the remainder and had 80 bricks left. How many bricks did he have at first?

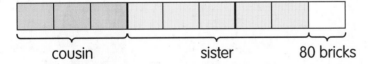

cousin   sister   80 bricks

The model above shows that:

1 unit ⟶ ☐ bricks

☐ units ⟶ 9 × ☐ = ☐ bricks

Nick had ☐ bricks at first.

Let's Practise!

Solve these word problems. Show your workings clearly.

7 Jane had 288 charity raffle tickets. She sold $\frac{2}{9}$ of the tickets to her relatives and $\frac{1}{3}$ of them to her friends.

    a How many tickets were sold to her relatives and friends?

    b How many tickets were not sold?

8 Miss Carpenter had £960. She spent $\frac{1}{4}$ of it on a holiday and $\frac{1}{6}$ of the remainder on a wetsuit. She kept the rest of the money. How much money did she keep?

9 Josh took 1 h 40 mins to complete a 3-lap race. He took $\frac{1}{4}$ of the total time to run the first lap and $\frac{1}{3}$ of the remaining time to run the second lap. The rest of the time was used to run the third lap. How many minutes did he take to run the third lap of the race?

10 Mr Young had a length of rope. He used $\frac{1}{4}$ of it to tie some boxes together. He then used $\frac{5}{9}$ of the remainder to make a skipping rope for his daughter. 120 cm of rope was left. What was the length of rope used to tie the boxes together?

11  Jeremy had a total of 216 photos of butterflies, bees and beetles in his collection. $\frac{7}{12}$ of the photos were butterflies, $\frac{5}{9}$ of the remainder were bees and the rest were beetles. How many photos of beetles were there in his collection?

Let's Practise!

12 Rhys bought a bag of assorted berries containing strawberries, raspberries and blueberries. $\frac{1}{4}$ of the berries were strawberries, $\frac{2}{3}$ of the remainder were raspberries and the rest were blueberries. If there were 48 raspberries, how many blueberries were there?

Practice Book 5A, p.113

Maths Journal

13 Tom and Selina did the following incorrectly. Explain and correct their mistakes.

a Tom: $\frac{2}{9} \div 3 = \frac{2}{3}$

b Selina: $\frac{2}{9} \times \frac{4}{11} = \frac{6}{20}$

Let's Wrap It Up!

You have learnt to:

- find the product of proper fractions
- find the product of an improper fraction and a proper or improper fraction
- find the product of a mixed number and a whole number using a calculator
- divide a proper fraction by a whole number.

Let's Wrap It Up!

Let's Revise!

Jody has a rectangular piece of material $\frac{7}{8}$ m long and $\frac{4}{5}$ m wide. She decides to share the rectangular piece of material equally with her friend.

a What is the area of the rectangular piece of material?

Method 1

$$\frac{7}{8} \times \frac{4}{5} = \frac{7 \times 4}{8 \times 5}$$

$$= \frac{28}{40}$$

$$= \frac{7}{10} \text{m}^2$$

The area of the rectangular piece of material is $\frac{7}{10}$ m².

Method 2

$$\frac{7}{8} \times \frac{4}{5} = \frac{7}{\cancel{8}_2} \times \frac{\cancel{4}^1}{5}$$

$$= \frac{7}{10} \text{m}^2$$

The area of the rectangular piece of material is $\frac{7}{10}$ m².

b What is the area of the piece of material her friend gets?

$$\frac{7}{10} \div 2 = \frac{7}{10} \times \frac{1}{2}$$

$$= \frac{7}{20} \text{m}^2$$

The area of the piece of material her friend gets is $\frac{7}{20}$ m².

Put On Your Thinking Caps!

14 Find the missing mass in each pattern.

a   2000 g $\frac{1}{3}$ of 18 kg   18 000 g   ☐ kg $\frac{1}{3}$ of 486 kg

b   7000 g   ☐ g $\frac{1}{12}$ of 228 kg   31 kg $1\frac{1}{4}$ of 37 600 g

15 In a race, Daniel was in 31st position. His position in the group was just behind $\frac{5}{9}$ of the children. How many children were in the race?

16 Keith bought 10 identical toy cars. Aisha bought $1\frac{1}{2}$ times as many of these toy cars as Keith. The total cost of the toy cars the two children had was £75. What was the cost of each toy car?

Practice Book 5A, p.117   Practice Book 5A, p.118

Unit 5 Area of a Triangle

Let's Learn!

Base and height of a triangle

1 ABC is a triangle.

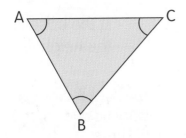

Let's recall the parts of a triangle. It has three sides and three angles.

The three sides are AB, BC and CA.

2 In triangle ABC:

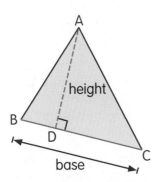

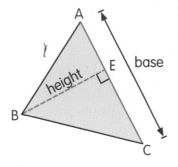

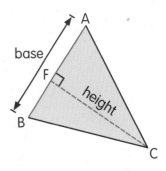

AD is perpendicular to BC. BC is called the **base** and AD is called the **height**.

BE is perpendicular to AC. In this case, AC is the base and BE is the height.

CF is perpendicular to AB. In this case, AB is the base and CF is the height.

133

3 PQR is another triangle.

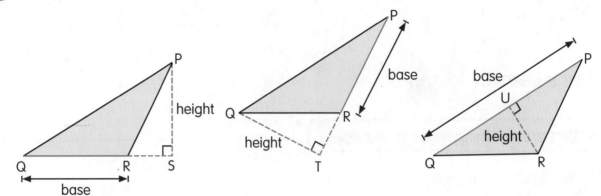

If the base is QR,
the height is PS.

If the base is PR,
the height is QT.

If the base is QP,
the height is RU.

Any side of a
triangle can
be the base.

The height is always
perpendicular to
the base.

4 Each of these triangles is named XYZ.

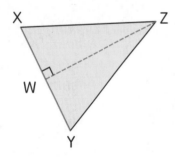

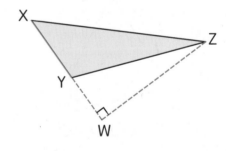

☐ is perpendicular to XY.
In each case, ☐ is the height and ☐ is the base.

5 Name the base for the given height in each triangle.

a

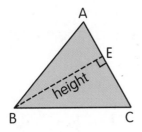

If the height is BE,
the base is ⬭.

b

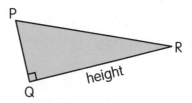

If the height is QR,
the base is ⬭.

c

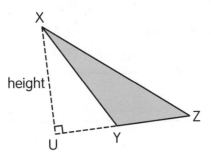

If the height is XU,
the base is ⬭.

6 Name the height for the given base in each triangle.

a

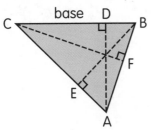

If the base is CB,
the height is ⬭.

b

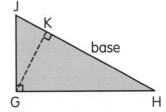

If the base is JH,
the height is ⬭.

c

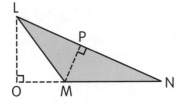

If the base is MN,
the height is ⬭.

d

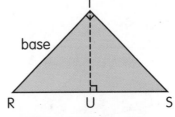

If the base is RT,
the height is ⬭.

Activity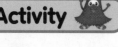

7 Work in groups.
Each person in your group draws a triangle and labels it ABC.
For example,

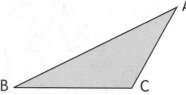

or

For each base AB, BC and CA, identify their heights.
Using a set-square, draw the three heights of your triangle and label
them AD, BE and CF. For each height, name the base.

Look at all the triangles drawn by the group.
What do you notice about the heights AD, BE and CF?

Let's Practise!

8 If the height is AD, what is the base?

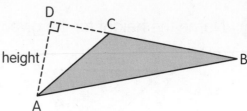

9 Copy the triangle and mark its height.

base

10 In triangle ABC:

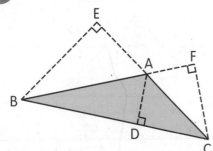

a if the base is ⬚, the height is ⬚.

b if the base is ⬚, the height is ⬚.

c if the base is ⬚, the height is ⬚.

Practice Book 5A, p.133

Let's Learn!

Finding the area of a triangle

1 What is the area of triangle ABC?

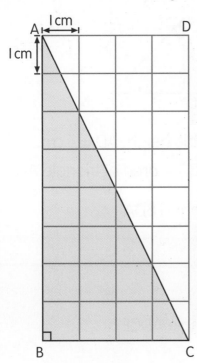

Triangle ABC is half of rectangle ABCD.

Recall that:
Area of a rectangle
= Length × Width.

ABCD is a rectangle.
In triangle ABC, AB is perpendicular to BC.
BC is the base when AB is the height.
The base BC = 4 cm and the height AB = 8 cm.

Area of triangle ABC = $\frac{1}{2}$ × area of rectangle ABCD

$\qquad\qquad\qquad\quad = \frac{1}{2} \times 4 \times 8 = 16\,cm^2$

How are the lengths 4 cm and 8 cm of rectangle ABCD related to triangle ABC?

They are the base and height of triangle ABC.

2 What is the area of triangle ABC?

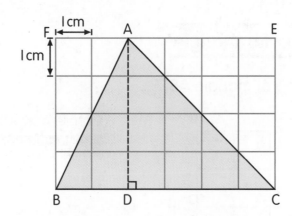

In triangle ABC, the base BC = 6 cm and the height AD = 4 cm.

Area of triangle ABC = area of triangle ABD + area of triangle ADC

Area of triangle ABD = $\frac{1}{2}$ × area of rectangle FBDA

$= \frac{1}{2}$ × 2 × 4

$= 4\,cm^2$

Area of triangle ADC = $\frac{1}{2}$ × area of rectangle ADCE

$= \frac{1}{2}$ × 4 × 4

$= 8\,cm^2$

So area of triangle ABC = 4 + 8

$= \boxed{12\,cm^2}$

Now area of rectangle FBCE = 6 × 4

$= 24\,cm^2$

Half of its area = $\boxed{12\,cm^2}$

So area of triangle ABC = $\frac{1}{2}$ × area of rectangle FBCE

$= \frac{1}{2}$ × 6 × 4

$= \frac{1}{2}$ × base BC × height AD

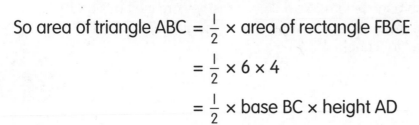

The lengths 6 cm and 4 cm of rectangle FBCE are the base and height of triangle ABC.

Triangle ABC is half of rectangle FBCE.

3 What is the area of triangle ABC?

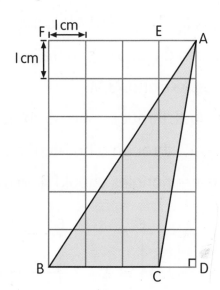

In triangle ABC, the base BC = 3 cm and the height AD = 6 cm.

Area of triangle ABC = area of triangle ABD – area of triangle ACD

Area of triangle ABD = $\frac{1}{2}$ × 4 × 6

= 12 cm^2

Area of triangle ACD = $\frac{1}{2}$ × 1 × 6

= 3 cm^2

So area of triangle ABC = 12 – 3

= 9 cm^2

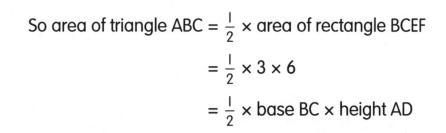

How are the lengths 3 cm and 6 cm of rectangle BCEF related to triangle ABC?

Now area of rectangle BCEF = 3 × 6

= 18 cm^2

Half of its area = 9 cm^2

So area of triangle ABC = $\frac{1}{2}$ × area of rectangle BCEF

= $\frac{1}{2}$ × 3 × 6

= $\frac{1}{2}$ × base BC × height AD

Activity

4   In triangle ABC, BC is the base and AD is the height.

    I   Copy Diagram I on a piece of square grid paper.

    2   Cut out triangles AKL and ALM.

    3   Rotate triangle AML through a half-turn about point M.

    4   Rotate triangle AKL through a half-turn about point K.

    5   The position of the triangles should now match Diagram 2.

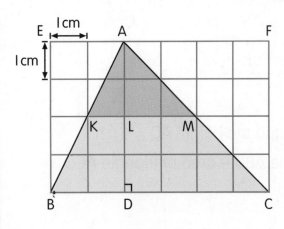

Diagram I

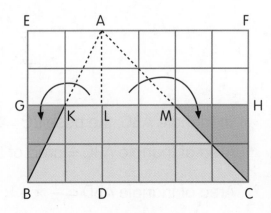

Diagram 2

Area of triangle ABC = area of rectangle ⬭

$$= \frac{1}{2} \times \text{area of rectangle } ⬭$$

$$= \frac{1}{2} \times BC \times EB$$

$$= \frac{1}{2} \times BC \times ⬭$$

$$= \frac{1}{2} \times \text{base} \times ⬭$$

Activity

5 In triangle PQR, QR is the base and PS is the height.

1 Copy Diagram 1 on a piece of square grid paper.

2 Cut out triangles PVX and VRX.

3 Rearrange the two triangles as shown in Diagram 2.

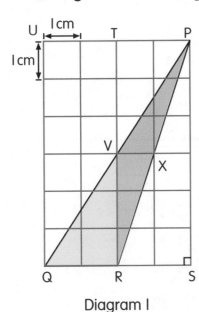  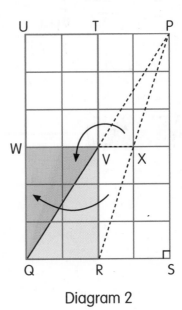

Diagram 1   Diagram 2

Area of triangle PQR = area of rectangle ⬭

$= \frac{1}{2} \times$ area of rectangle ⬭

$= \frac{1}{2} \times QR \times TR$

$= \frac{1}{2} \times QR \times$ ⬭

$= \frac{1}{2} \times$ base $\times$ ⬭

Area of a triangle $= \frac{1}{2} \times$ Base $\times$ Height

6 Find the area of triangle PQR.

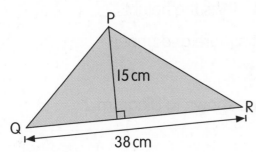

Area of triangle PQR $= \frac{1}{2} \times$ base $\times$ height

$= \frac{1}{2} \times 38 \times 15$

$=$ ⬚

Activity

7

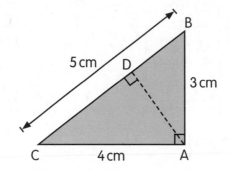

Work in pairs.

ABC is a triangle. ∠BAC is a right angle and AD is perpendicular to BC.

1 Measure the height AD in centimetres to 1 decimal place.

2 In turn, take each side of the triangle, AB, AC, BC as the base.

3 Work out the area of triangle ABC. Do you get the same area?

8 Find the area of each shaded triangle.

a

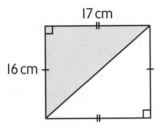

17 cm
16 cm

b

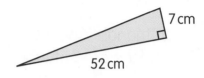

7 cm
52 cm

c

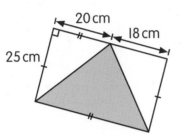

20 cm
18 cm
25 cm

d

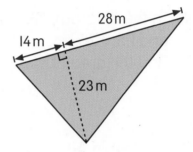

28 m
14 m
23 m

e

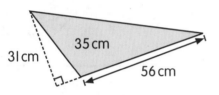

35 cm
31 cm
56 cm

f

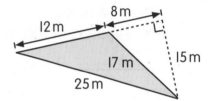

8 m
12 m
17 m
15 m
25 m

Let's Practise!

9 Find the area of each shaded triangle.

a

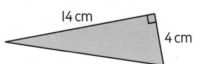

14 cm
4 cm

b

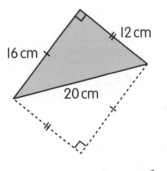

12 cm
16 cm
20 cm

c

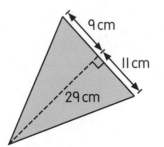

9 cm
11 cm
29 cm

d

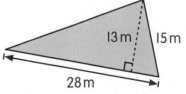

13 m
15 m
28 m

Let's Practise!

10 In triangle ABC, BC = 44 cm and AD = 27 cm.
    Find the area of triangle ABC.

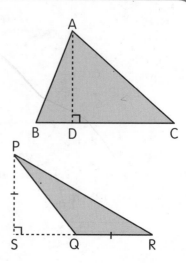

11 In the diagram, QR = 26 cm, QS = 20 cm
    and PS = 26 cm.
    Find the area of triangle PQR.

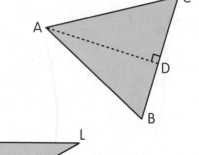

12 In triangle ABC, BD = 9 m, DC = 10 m
    and AD = 18 m.
    Find the area of triangle ABC.

13 In the diagram, LM = 18 cm,
    KM = 16 cm and KN = 14 cm.
    Find the area of triangle KLM.

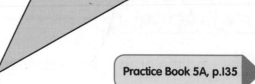

Practice Book 5A, p.135

Maths Journal

14

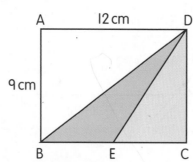

ABCD is a rectangle and BE = EC.
What can you say about the areas of triangles BED and ECD? Why?

Let's Explore!

15

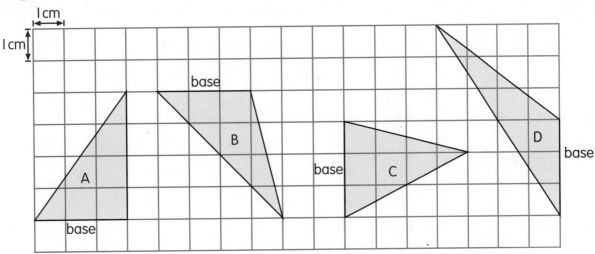

For each triangle above, find the height. Then find its area.
What can you say about the bases and heights of these triangles?

Complete this statement:

Different triangles with equal bases and equal ⬭ have the same ⬭.

Let's Wrap It Up!

You have learnt:

- to identify the three sides of a triangle
- that any side of a triangle can be the base
- that the height of a triangle is always perpendicular to the base
- **Area of a triangle = $\frac{1}{2}$ × Base × Height**.

Let's Wrap It Up!

Let's Revise!

ABCD is a rectangle of perimeter 48 cm. AB = 6 cm and CD = DE.

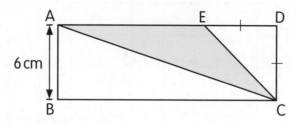

a Find the length of the rectangle.
Perimeter = 48 cm
AB + BC = 48 ÷ 2
          = 24 cm
Length BC = 24 − 6
          = 18 cm

b Find the area of the shaded triangle ACE.

Method 1
DE = CD = 6 cm
AD = BC = 18 cm
Area of △CDE = $\frac{1}{2}$ × 6 × 6
                = 18 cm²
Area of △ACD = $\frac{1}{2}$ × 18 × 6
                = 54 cm²
Area of shaded triangle ACE = Area of △ACD − Area of △CDE
                            = 54 − 18
                            = 36 cm²

Method 2
Area of shaded triangle ACE = $\frac{1}{2}$ × AE × CD
                = $\frac{1}{2}$ × (18 − 6) × 6
                = $\frac{1}{2}$ × 12 × 6
                = 36 cm²

Put On Your Thinking Caps!

16 ABCD is a rectangle. BE = ED.

Find the area of the shaded triangle ABE.

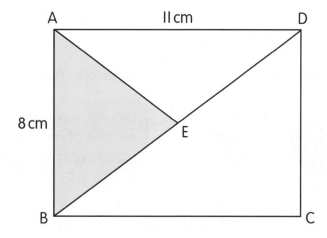

Practice Book 5A, p.140   Practice Book 5A, p.142

Unit 6 Ratio

Let's Learn!

 Finding ratio

1 There are 2 chocolate muffins and 1 blueberry muffin.

> Let's compare the number of chocolate muffins with the number of blueberry muffins.

The **ratio** of the number of **chocolate muffins to** the number of **blueberry muffins** is **2 : 1**.

> We read 2 : 1 as **2 to 1**.

> Here the ratio gives the number of objects in each set.

The **ratio** of the number of **blueberry muffins to** the number of **chocolate muffins** is **1 : 2**.

2

The ratio of the number of **blue flags** to the number of **yellow flags** is ◯ : ◯.

The ratio of the number of **yellow flags** to the number of **blue flags** is ◯ : ◯.

3 Meena has 2 trays of large eggs and 3 trays of small eggs.

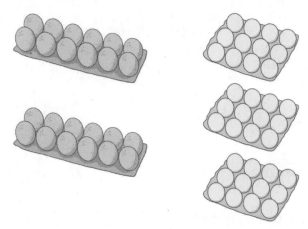

There is an equal number of eggs on each tray.

The ratio of the number of large eggs to the number of small eggs is 2 : 3.

2 trays to 3 trays is 2 : 3.

The ratio of the number of small eggs to the number of large eggs is 3 : 2.

I tray contains 12 eggs. Here the ratio does not give the actual numbers of large and small eggs.

4

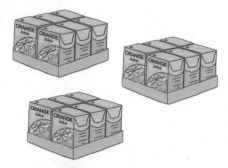

The ratio of the number of boxes of orange juice to the number of boxes of apple juice is ⬜ : ⬜.

The ratio of the number of boxes of apple juice to the number of boxes of orange juice is ⬜ : ⬜.

5   Tim bought 2 kg of onions and 9 kg of potatoes.

To compare as a ratio, the masses must be in the same unit.

The ratio of the mass of potatoes to the mass of onions is ⬭ : ⬭ .

The ratio of the mass of onions to the mass of potatoes is ⬭ : ⬭ .

6

I unit

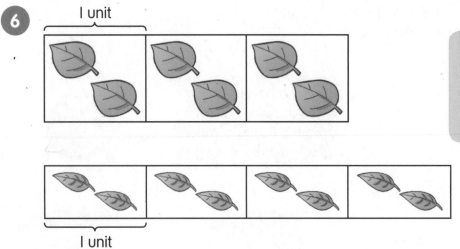

I unit

I unit = 2 leaves
So a ratio does not necessarily give the actual quantities compared.

The ratio of the number of big leaves to the number of small leaves is 3 : 4.

The ratio of the number of small leaves to the number of big leaves is ⬭ : ⬭ .

7

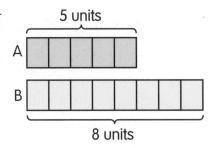

A

5 units

B

8 units

5 units to 8 units

The ratio of the length of A to the length of B is 5 : 8.

The ratio of the length of B to the length of A is ⬭ : ⬭.

8 Alison cuts a piece of wood, 24 cm long, into two. The shorter piece is 7 cm long. Find the ratio of the length of the shorter piece to the length of the longer piece.

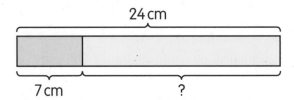

24 cm

7 cm   ?

Length of shorter piece of wood = 7 cm

Length of longer piece of wood = 24 – 7

= 17 cm

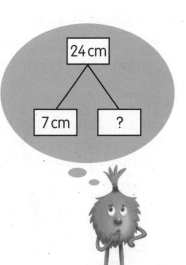

24 cm

7 cm   ?

The ratio of the length of the shorter piece to the length of the longer piece is 7 : 17.

9 Matt had 15 kg of rice. He sold 7 kg of the rice. What was the ratio of the mass of rice sold to the mass of rice left?

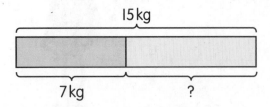

Mass of rice sold = ⬡ kg

Mass of rice left = ⬡ – ⬡

= ⬡ kg

The ratio of the mass of rice sold to the mass of rice left is ⬡ : ⬡.

Let's Explore!

10 Work in pairs.

You will need 10 cubes.

1 First separate the 10 cubes into two groups. Count the number of cubes in each group.

2 Record your answers in a table as shown below.

Group A	Group B	Ratio A : B
1	9	1 : 9
2	8	2 : 8
⋮	⋮	⋮

3 Next join the cubes in 2s. Then put them in two groups. Count the units of cubes in each group.

4 Record your answers in the same way as in **2**.

Group A	Group B	Ratio A : B
2	8	2 : 8
4	6	4 : 6
⋮	⋮	⋮

5 Discuss the ratios obtained in the two tables.

Let's Practise!

11 The table shows the masses of seafood sold by a fishmonger.

Seafood	Mussels	Prawns	Lobsters	Crabs	Crayfish
Mass	2 kg	5 kg	3 kg	11 kg	8 kg

Copy and complete the table below. Then write as many ratios as you can from the data given above. An example is shown.

	Ratio
Mass of mussels to mass of prawns	2 : 5
Mass of lobsters to mass of crayfish	⬭ : ⬭
⋮	⋮
Mass of crabs to total mass of seafood	⬭ : ⬭

12 Draw models to show the following ratios.

Example

A : B = 2 : 5

A [   ][   ]
B [ ][ ][ ][ ][ ]

a A : B = 4 : 9   **b** A : B = 11 : 7
c A : B = 8 : 3   **d** A : B = 12 : 5

13 Look at the pictures below. Write two ratios to compare the number of eggs in Set A and in Set B.

Set A   Set B

Let's Practise!

14 Look at the picture below. Write two ratios to compare the items shown.

I unit

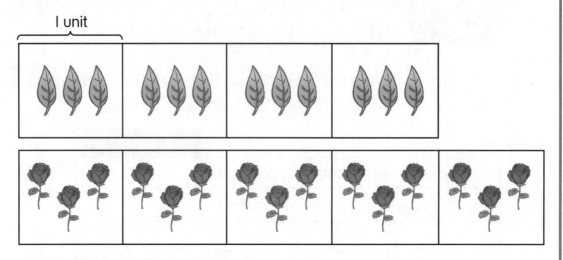

15 A huge chequered table cloth is 3 m wide and 7 m long. Find the ratio of the length of the table cloth to its width.

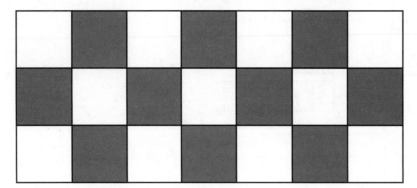

16 Mr Bell has £88. He gives £35 to his son and the rest to his daughter. Find the ratio of the amount of money his son gets to the amount of money his daughter gets.

Practice Book 5A, p.143

Let's Learn!

Equivalent ratios

1 Ella has 4 red apples and 8 green apples. The ratio of the number of red apples to the number of green apples is 4 : 8. Ella puts 2 apples of the same colour on each tray.

2 trays of red apples

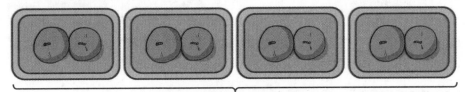

4 trays of green apples

= 1 unit

There are 2 trays of red apples and 4 trays of green apples.

The ratio of the number of red apples to the number of green apples is 2 : 4.

Next she puts 4 apples of the same colour on each tray.

= 1 unit

1 tray of
red apples

2 trays of green apples

There is 1 tray of red apples and 2 trays of green apples.

The ratio of the number of red apples to the number of green apples
is 1 : 2.

The three ratios 4 : 8, 2 : 4 and 1 : 2 compare the same number of red
apples and green apples.

These ratios are **equivalent ratios**:

4 : 8 = 2 : 4 = 1 : 2

1 : 2 is a ratio in its **simplest form**.

Which ratio shows the actual number of red apples and green apples?

2

The ratio of the number of pencils to the number of board pins
is ⬚ : ⬚.

⬚ groups of pencils   ⬚ groups of board pins

The ratio of the number of pencils to the number of board pins
is ⬚ : ⬚.

⬚ group of pencils   ⬚ groups of board pins

The ratio of the number of pencils to the number of board pins
is ⬚ : ⬚.

The equivalent ratios are ⬚ : ⬚ , ⬚ : ⬚ and ⬚ : ⬚.

In these equivalent ratios, the ratio in its simplest form is ⬚ : ⬚.

The ratio which shows the actual number of pencils and
board pins is ⬚ : ⬚.

3 What is the ratio 4 : 6 in its simplest form?

$2 \times 2 = 4$ and $2 \times 3 = 6$.
2 is a common factor of 4 and 6.

Divide 4 and 6 by 2.

4 : 6

$\div 2$ ( ) $\div 2$

= **2 : 3**

2 and 3 cannot be divided further by a common factor.

The ratio 4 : 6 in its simplest form is 2 : 3.

4 What is each ratio in its simplest form?

a   12 : 4

$\div$ ⬭ ( ) $\div$ ⬭

= ⬭ : ⬭

⬭ is a common factor of 12 and 4. Divide 12 and 4 by ⬭.

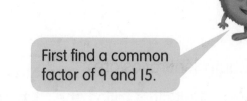

b   9 : 15

$\div$ ⬭ ( ) $\div$ ⬭

= ⬭ : ⬭

First find a common factor of 9 and 15.

5 Find the missing number in these equivalent ratios.

$2 : 5 = 6 : \boxed{}$

Look at the first terms of the equivalent ratios – $\mathbf{2} : 5 = \mathbf{6} : \boxed{}$.

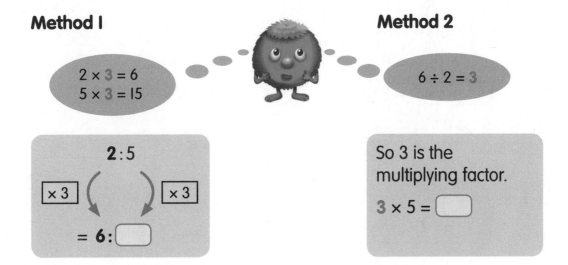

Method I

$2 \times 3 = 6$
$5 \times 3 = 15$

$\mathbf{2} : 5$

$\boxed{\times 3}$ ⟲⟳ $\boxed{\times 3}$

$= \mathbf{6} : \boxed{}$

Method 2

$6 \div 2 = 3$

So 3 is the multiplying factor.

$3 \times 5 = \boxed{}$

6 Find the missing number in these equivalent ratios.

$15 : 12 = \boxed{} : 4$

Look at the second terms of the equivalent ratios – $15 : \mathbf{12} = \boxed{} : \mathbf{4}$.

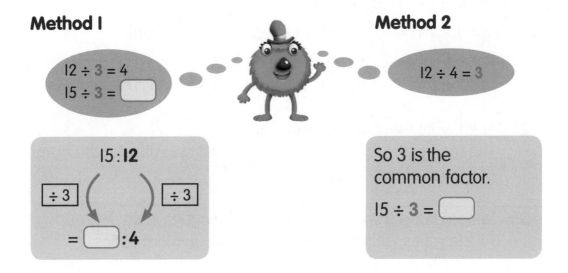

Method I

$12 \div 3 = 4$
$15 \div 3 = \boxed{}$

$15 : \mathbf{12}$

$\boxed{\div 3}$ ⟲⟳ $\boxed{\div 3}$

$= \boxed{} : \mathbf{4}$

Method 2

$12 \div 4 = 3$

So 3 is the common factor.

$15 \div 3 = \boxed{}$

7 Find the missing number in these equivalent ratios.

a
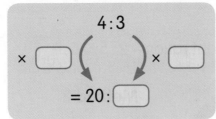

$20 \div 4 = \boxed{}$

$3 \times 5 = \boxed{}$

b
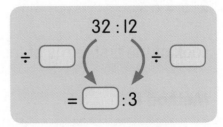

$12 \div 3 = \boxed{}$

$32 \div 4 = \boxed{}$

c

$7 : \boxed{}$

$= 21 : 12$

$21 \div 7 = \boxed{}$

$12 \div 3 = \boxed{}$

d

$\boxed{} : 16$

$= 3 : 2$

$16 \div 2 = \boxed{}$

$3 \times 8 = \boxed{}$

Activity

8 Work in groups of two or four.

Each group will need 14 yellow cubes and 28 red cubes.

1 Put the cubes in groups so that each group has the same number of cubes. You cannot mix yellow cubes and red cubes in a group.

2 Then write the ratio as shown below.
The ratio of the number of groups of yellow cubes to the number of groups of red cubes is $\boxed{} : \boxed{}$.

3 Repeat **1** and **2** with a new number of cubes in each group.
All the ratios you have obtained are **equivalent ratios**.

4 You can repeat the activity using 8 yellow cubes and 24 red cubes.

Let's Practise!

Answer these questions.

9 Mr Lee had 3 boxes of red chalk and 8 boxes of white chalk.
Each box contained 5 pieces of chalk.

    a Find the number of pieces of red chalk Mr Lee had.

    b How many pieces of white chalk did Mr Lee have?

    c Find the ratio of the number of pieces of red chalk to the number of pieces of white chalk.

    d Find the ratio of the number of boxes of red chalk to the number of boxes of white chalk.

    e What can you say about the ratios in **c** and **d** ?

10 Express each of the following ratios in its simplest form.

    a $4:14 = \boxed{}:\boxed{}$ **b** $18:8 = \boxed{}:\boxed{}$

    c $8:32 = \boxed{}:\boxed{}$ **d** $42:12 = \boxed{}:\boxed{}$

11 Complete the equivalent ratios.

    a $4:7 = 12:\boxed{}$ **b** $3:8 = \boxed{}:32$

    c $27:15 = \boxed{}:5$ **d** $6:42 = 2:\boxed{}$

12 Complete the equivalent ratios.

    a $3:\boxed{} = 48:80$ **b** $\boxed{}:51 = 4:3$

    c $70:\boxed{} = 2:4$ **d** $\boxed{}:7 = 128:224$

Practice Book 5A, p.147

Let's Learn!

Word problems (I)

1 There are 6 goats and 18 cows on Joseph's farm. Find the ratio of the number of goats to the number of cows on his farm.

The ratio of the number of goats to the number of cows is 6 : 18.

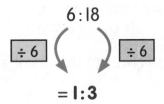

Write the ratio 6 : 18 in its simplest form. Divide 6 and 18 by the common factor, 6.

The ratio of the number of goats to the number of cows on the farm is 1 : 3.

2 There are 12 pink roses and 15 yellow roses in Amit's garden. Find the ratio of:

a the number of pink roses to the number of yellow roses

b the number of yellow roses to the number of pink roses

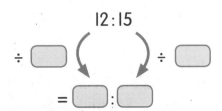

Write the ratio 12 : 15 in its simplest form. Divide 12 and 15 by the common factor, 3.

a The ratio of the number of pink roses to the number of yellow roses is ⬚ : ⬚ in its simplest form.

b The ratio of the number of yellow roses to the number of pink roses is ⬚ : ⬚.

3 48 children attend a party. 16 of them are girls. Find the ratio of the number of girls to the number of boys at the party.

48 − 16 = 32

There are 32 boys at the party.

16 : 32 = 1 : 2

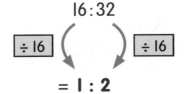

16 : 32

÷ 16   ÷ 16

= 1 : 2

The ratio of the number of girls to the number of boys at the party is 1 : 2.

4 On a rainy day, Mr Jones sold 56 umbrellas and raincoats altogether. He sold 24 raincoats on that day.

a Find the ratio of the total number of umbrellas and raincoats sold to the number of raincoats sold.

b Find the ratio of the number of umbrellas sold to the number of raincoats sold.

a ⬚ : ⬚ = ⬚ : ⬚

The ratio of the total number of umbrellas and raincoats sold to the number of raincoats sold is ⬚ : ⬚.

b Number of umbrellas sold = ⬚ − ⬚

= ⬚

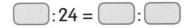

⬚ : 24 = ⬚ : ⬚

The ratio of the number of umbrellas sold to the number of raincoats sold is ⬚ : ⬚.

5 There are 25 plums and 40 grapes in a basket. Millie eats 5 grapes. What is the ratio of the number of plums to the number of grapes left in the basket now?

40 − 5 = 35 grapes
There are 35 grapes in the basket now.

25 : 35

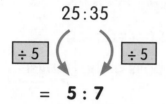

= **5 : 7**

The ratio of the number of plums to the number of grapes in the basket now is 5 : 7.

6 Roy bakes 30 apple pies and 16 strawberry tarts. He then bakes another 18 apple pies. Find the ratio of the number of apple pies to the number of strawberry tarts in the end.

30 + ⬚ = ⬚ apple pies
There are ⬚ apple pies in the end.

⬚ : 16 = ⬚ : ⬚

The ratio of the number of apple pies to the number of strawberry tarts in the end is ⬚ : ⬚.

7 A farm has 96 chickens and ducks altogether. 60 of them are chickens. What is the ratio of the number of chickens to the number of ducks?

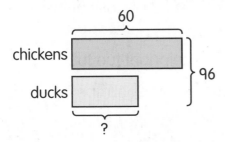

Number of ducks = 96 − 60 = 36

$60:36 = 5:3$

The ratio of the number of chickens to the number of ducks is $5:3$.

8 Sam collected a total of 252 wooden and plastic figures. 56 of them were plastic figures. What is the ratio of the number of wooden figures to the number of plastic figures?

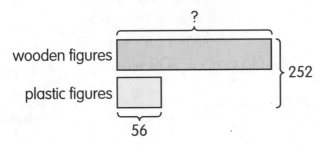

Number of wooden figures = ☐ − ☐ = ☐

☐ : ☐ = ☐ : ☐

The ratio of the number of wooden figures to the number of plastic figures is ☐ : ☐.

9 A fishmonger divides a box of prawns into two portions. The ratio of the mass of the bigger portion to the mass of the smaller portion is 5:2. The mass of the bigger portion is 15 kg. Find the mass of the smaller portion.

Method 1

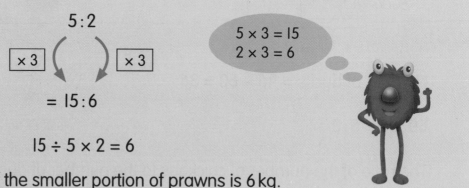

5:2

×3   ×3

= 15:6

$15 \div 5 \times 2 = 6$

The mass of the smaller portion of prawns is 6 kg.

5 × 3 = 15
2 × 3 = 6

Method 2

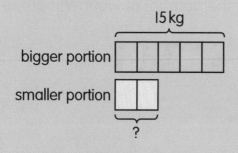

15 kg

bigger portion

smaller portion

?

We can also solve this problem using a model to represent the ratio 5:2 as 5 units to 2 units.

5 units → 15 kg
1 unit → 15 ÷ 5 = 3 kg
2 units → 2 × 3 = 6 kg

The mass of the smaller portion of prawns is 6 kg.

10 Charlotte has two bottles of milk. The ratio of the volume of milk in Bottle A to the volume of milk in Bottle B is 3:4. The volume of milk in Bottle A is 120 ml. Find the total volume of milk in both bottles.

Method 1

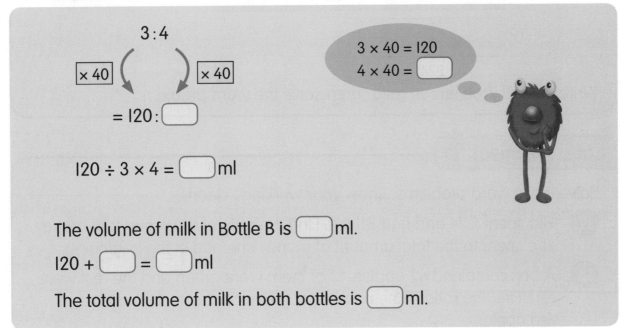

3:4

×40 ⟶ ⟵ ×40

= 120 : ◯

3 × 40 = 120
4 × 40 = ◯

120 ÷ 3 × 4 = ◯ ml

The volume of milk in Bottle B is ◯ ml.

120 + ◯ = ◯ ml

The total volume of milk in both bottles is ◯ ml.

Method 2

◯ ml

Bottle A

Bottle B

} ? ml

We can also draw a model to solve the same problem.

3 units ⟶ ◯ ml

1 unit ⟶ ◯ ÷ ◯ = ◯ ml

7 units ⟶ ◯ × ◯ = ◯ ml

The total volume of milk in both bottles is ◯ ml.

Maths Journal

11 Look at the model below.

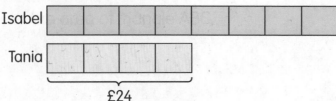

Isabel

Tania

£24

Write a word problem on ratio. Then solve the word problem.

Let's Practise!

Solve these word problems. Show your workings clearly.

12 Ella spent £24 and had £11 left. Find the ratio of the amount of money she spent to the total amount of money she had in the beginning.

13 A box contained 42 apples. 12 of them were green and the rest were red. Find the ratio of the number of green apples to the number of red apples.

14 Peter mixed flour and sugar in the ratio 5:2. If he used 125 g of flour, what was the mass of sugar he used?

15 Mr White cuts a coil of wire into two pieces in the ratio 3:4. If the length of the longer piece of wire is 32 cm, what is the total length of the wire?

16 The ratio of the number of pupils at the park in the morning to the number of pupils at the park in the afternoon was 13:7.
143 pupils were at the park in the morning. What was the number of pupils at the park in the afternoon?

17 Vanessa cuts a piece of rope into two, in the ratio 19:4.
The length of the longer piece is 266 cm. What is the length of the shorter piece of rope?

18 The total time that Emily and Bob worked in two weeks was 91 h.
If Emily worked 52 h, what was the ratio of Emily working hours to Bob's working hours?

Practice Book 5A, p.149

Let's Learn!

Comparing three quantities

1 Mrs Wolfe had 4 red roses, 8 pink roses and 12 yellow roses. The ratio of the number of red roses to the number of pink roses to the number of yellow roses is 4 : 8 : 12.

Method 1

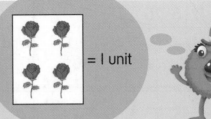

= 1 unit

She puts 4 roses into each box.

1 box of red roses   2 boxes of pink roses   3 boxes of yellow roses

The ratio of the number of red roses to the number of pink roses to the number of yellow roses is 1 : 2 : 3.

Method 2

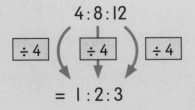

$$4 : 8 : 12$$
$$\div 4 \quad \div 4 \quad \div 4$$
$$= 1 : 2 : 3$$

4 is a common factor of 4, 8 and 12.

4 : 8 : 12 is 1 : 2 : 3 in its simplest form.

The ratio of the number of red roses to the number of pink roses to the number of yellow roses is ☐ : ☐ : ☐.

2 What is each ratio in its simplest form?

a   15 : 12 : 18

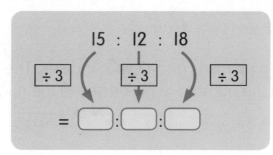

Divide 15, 12 and 18 by the common factor, 3.

b   12 : 8 : 20

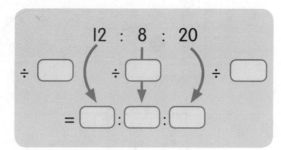

First find the common factor of 12, 8 and 20.

3 Find the missing numbers in these equivalent ratios.

2 : 3 : 5 = ⬚ : 12 : ⬚

Look at the second terms of the equivalent ratios –

2 : **3** : 5 = ⬚ : **12** : ⬚ .

First find the multiplying factor. Then multiply the first and third terms by the multiplying factor.

Method 1

$3 \times 4 = 12$
Multiply by 4 throughout.

2 : **3** : 5

× 4   × 4   × 4

= ⬚ : **12** : ⬚

Method 2

$12 \div 3 = 4$

So 4 is the multiplying factor.

$4 \times 2 = ⬚$

$4 \times 5 = ⬚$

4 Find the missing numbers in these equivalent ratios.

$3 : 5 : 7 = 9 : \boxed{} : \boxed{}$

Look at the first terms of the equivalent ratios – $3 : 5 : 7 = 9 : \boxed{} : \boxed{}$.

First find the multiplying factor. Then multiply the second and third terms by the multiplying factor.

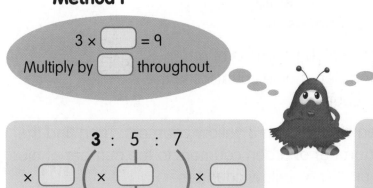

Method 1

$3 \times \boxed{} = 9$

Multiply by $\boxed{}$ throughout.

$$\begin{array}{ccccc} \mathbf{3} & : & 5 & : & 7 \\ \times \boxed{} & \left(\times \boxed{} \right. & & \left. \times \boxed{} \right) \\ = & \mathbf{9} & : \boxed{} & : \boxed{} \end{array}$$

Method 2

$9 \div 3 = \boxed{}$

So $\boxed{}$ is the multiplying factor.

$3 \times 5 = \boxed{}$

$3 \times 7 = \boxed{}$

5 Find the missing numbers in these equivalent ratios.

$18 : 12 : 9 = \boxed{} : \boxed{} : 3$

Look at the third terms of the equivalent ratios –

$18 : 12 : \mathbf{9} = \boxed{} : \boxed{} : \mathbf{3}$

First find the common factor. Then divide the first and second terms by the common factor.

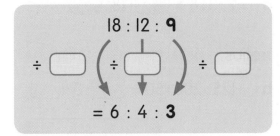

$$\begin{array}{ccccc} 18 & : & 12 & : & \mathbf{9} \\ \div \boxed{} & \left(\div \boxed{} \right. & & \left. \div \boxed{} \right) \\ = & 6 & : 4 & : & \mathbf{3} \end{array}$$

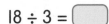

$9 \div 3 = 3$

So $\boxed{}$ is the common factor.

$18 \div 3 = \boxed{}$

$12 \div 3 = \boxed{}$

6 Find the missing numbers in these equivalent ratios.

a $15:5:20 = $ ⬚ $:1:$ ⬚

b $7:21:14 = $ ⬚ $:$ ⬚ $:2$

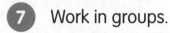

Activity

7 Work in groups.

Each group will need 3 green counters, 12 blue counters and 27 yellow counters.

a Write down the ratio of the number of green counters to the number of blue counters to the number of yellow counters.

b Take away 1 green counter and 3 yellow counters. Then find the new ratio of the number of green counters to the number of blue counters to the number of yellow counters.

Let's Practise!

Find the missing numbers in the following equivalent ratios.

8 Write each ratio in its simplest form.

a $5:15:20 = $ ⬚ $:$ ⬚ $:$ ⬚

b $4:18:24 = $ ⬚ $:$ ⬚ $:$ ⬚

c $15:75:135 = $ ⬚ $:$ ⬚ $:$ ⬚

d $36:54:108 = $ ⬚ $:$ ⬚ $:$ ⬚

9 Complete each set of equivalent ratios.

a $1:4:5 = 3:$ ⬚ $:$ ⬚

b $2:3:8 = $ ⬚ $:18:$ ⬚

10 🖩 Complete each set of equivalent ratios.

a $64:112:32 = $ ⬚ $:$ ⬚ $:2$

b $125:200:50 = $ ⬚ $:8:$ ⬚

Practice Book 5A, p.153 ▶

Let's Learn!

Word problems (2)

1 At a toy shop, Bill bought 3 pink toy cars, 6 blue toy cars, and 9 yellow toy cars. What was the ratio of the number of pink toy cars to the number of blue toy cars to the number of yellow toy cars that Bill bought?

Method 1

Put 3 toy cars into each box.

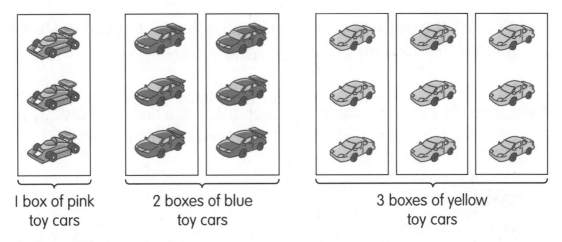

| 1 box of pink toy cars | 2 boxes of blue toy cars | 3 boxes of yellow toy cars |

The ratio of the number of pink toy cars to the number of blue toy cars to the number of yellow toy cars that Bill bought was $1:2:3$.

Method 2

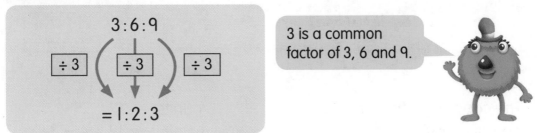

3 is a common factor of 3, 6 and 9.

$3:6:9$ is $1:2:3$ in its simplest form.

The ratio of the number of pink toy cars to the number of blue toy cars to the number of yellow toy cars that Bill bought was ⬜ : ⬜ : ⬜.

2 During a race, Daniel ran 200 m, Hardeep ran 800 m and Omar ran 3000 m. What was the ratio of the distance Daniel ran to the distance Hardeep ran to the distance Omar ran?

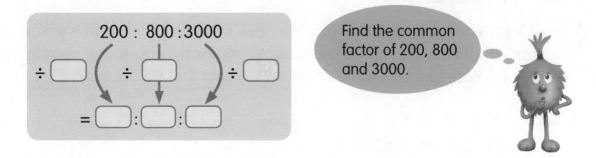

Find the common factor of 200, 800 and 3000.

The ratio of the distance Daniel ran to the distance Hardeep ran to the distance Omar ran was ⬭ : ⬭ : ⬭.

3 Rebecca filled three containers, A, B and C, to the brim with orange juice in the ratio 2:3:4. The capacity of the largest container was 12 ℓ. Find the capacity of the smallest container.

Method 1

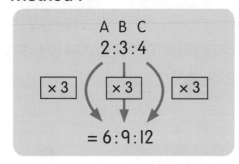

The capacity of the smallest container is 6 ℓ.

Method 2

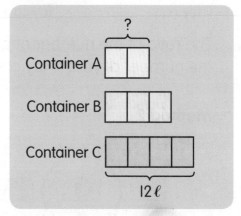

4 units ⟶ 12 ℓ
1 unit ⟶ 12 ÷ 4 = 3 ℓ
2 units ⟶ 2 × 3 = 6 ℓ

The capacity of the smallest container is 6 ℓ.

4 Ray cut a roll of ribbon into three pieces, X, Y and Z, in the ratio of 4:2:1. The length of the longest piece is 28 m. Find the total length of the three pieces.

4 units ⟶ 28 m

1 unit ⟶ ⬭ ÷ ⬭ = ⬭ m

Total length = 4 + 2 + 1 units = ⬭ units

= ⬭ × ⬭ = ⬭ m

The total length of the three pieces is ⬭ m.

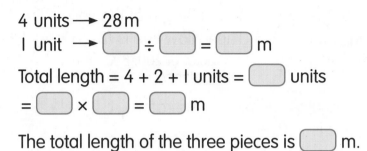

5 🧮 Mr Allen, Miss Brown and Mr Bishop shared a sum of money in the ratio 5:4:6. Mr Bishop's share of the money was £432. How much was the total amount of money?

6 units ⟶ £432

1 unit ⟶ £⬭ ÷ ⬭ = £⬭

Total amount of money

= 5 + 4 + 6 = ⬭ units

= ⬭ × ⬭

= £⬭

Mr Allen

Miss Brown

Mr Bishop

£432

The total amount of money was £⬭.

Let's Practise!

Solve these problems. Show your working clearly.

6 At a stationery shop, Mrs Chase bought 5 rubbers, 15 pens and 40 pencils. What was the ratio of the number of rubbers to the number of pens to the number of pencils that Mrs Chase bought at the stationery shop?

7 Anita mixes 200 ml of cranberry juice, 300 ml of grapefruit juice and 700 ml of lemonade for Angie's birthday party. What is the ratio of the amount of cranberry juice to that of grapefruit juice to that of lemonade?

Let's Practise!

8 Ron draws three lines in different colours – red, yellow and green. The ratio of the length of the red line to the length of the yellow line to the length of the green line is 1:3:5. The yellow line is 18 cm long. How long is the green line?

9 Apple, carrot and orange juice is mixed in the ratio 3:1:2. The volume of apple juice is 720 ml.

    a How much more apple juice is used in the mixture than carrot juice?

    b What is the total volume of the juice?

10 Mrs Evans, Mrs Bowden and Miss Harper share a sum of money in the ratio 2:4:15. Miss Harper has £1575.

    a Which girl gets the smallest share?

    b What is the total sum of money shared by Mrs Evans, Mrs Bowden and Miss Harper?

11 Ethan, George and Amit have some action figures in the ratio 13:5:7. Ethan has 65 action figures.

    a How many action figures does Amit have?

    b What is the total number of action figures that Ethan, George and Amit have?

Practice Book 5A, p.155

Maths Journal

12 Miya has 10 white balloons and 20 blue balloons.

Explain how to find the ratio of the number of white balloons to that of the blue balloons in its simplest form. Draw a model if you need to.

Let's Explore!

13 **a** Using the following numbers, write sets of equivalent ratios in the form *a* : *b*. You can use each number only once.

2 3 5 6 7 8 9 10 12 14 15 20 21 25 35

Example

$$2:3 = 6:9 = 8:12$$

b Using the same numbers in **a**, write as many sets of equivalent ratios in the form *a* : *b* : *c* as you can. You can use each number **only once**.

How many sets of equivalent ratios can you write for **a** and **b**?

How do you choose the numbers for each set of equivalent ratios? Discuss.

Let's Wrap It Up!

You have learnt:

- to use ratio to show the relative sizes of 2 quantities and 3 quantities
- that a given ratio does not necessarily give the actual quantities compared
- to find an equivalent ratio by multiplying the ratio by a common factor

1 : 4

× 4 ( ) × 4

= 4 : 16

- that a ratio can be reduced to its simplest form by dividing the ratio by the common factor.

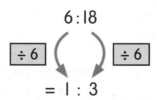

6 : 18

÷ 6 ( ) ÷ 6

= 1 : 3

Let's Wrap It Up!

Let's Revise!

The ratio of the perimeter of a square piece of paper to the perimeter of a rectangular piece of paper is 2 : 5. If each side of the square piece of paper is 10 cm, find:

a   the perimeter of the square piece of paper

10 × 4 = 40 cm

The perimeter of the square piece of paper is 40 cm.

b   the perimeter of the rectangular piece of paper

2 units ⟶ 40 cm
1 unit ⟶ 20 cm
5 units ⟶ 100 cm

The perimeter of the rectangular piece of paper is 100 cm.

c   the length of the rectangular piece of paper if its width is 15 cm.

Length of the rectangular piece of paper = $\dfrac{100 - (15 \times 2)}{2}$

$= 35$ cm

The length of the rectangular piece of paper is 35 cm.

Put On Your Thinking Caps!

14   Sam and Tina had some money in the ratio 5 : 2. Sam had £30. If Tina's money consisted only of 20 pence coins, how many 20 pence coins did Tina have?

15   Linda had some 50 pence coins and 20 pence coins in the ratio 3 : 2. Linda had four 20 pence coins. How much money did Linda have altogether?

Practice Book 5A, p.161   Practice Book 5A, p.162